VIEW OF MODERN MECCA.

MAHOMET AND ISLAM

MAHOMET AND ISLAM

A SKETCH OF THE PROPHET'S LIFE FROM ORIGINAL SOURCES, AND A BRIEF OUTLINE OF HIS RELIGION.

by

SIR WILLIAM MUIR,

K.C.S.I., LL.D. D.C.L.,

NEW AND REVISED EDITION.

With Light Illustrations and Map.

GYAN

Published by

Gyan Publishing House
5, Ansari Road
Daryaganj, New Delhi-110002
Phone: 011-47034999, 9811692060
E-mail: books@gyanbooks.com

Distribution Network
gyanbooks.com
India, USA, Canada, UK, Australia, France

ISBN : 978-81-212-6037-4 (PB)
First Published, 1887

2nd Impression 2021

Printed at: Gyan Press, Delhi.

Mahomet and Islam
Author: Sir William Muir

MAHOMET AND ISLAM

A SKETCH OF THE PROPHET'S LIFE FROM ORIGINAL SOURCES, AND A BRIEF OUTLINE OF HIS RELIGION.

BY

SIR WILLIAM MUIR, K.C.S.I., LL.D., D.C.L.,

AUTHOR OF

"THE LIFE OF MAHOMET," "THE EARLY CALIPHATE," "THE RISE AND DECLINE OF ISLAM," ETC.

NEW AND REVISED EDITION.

With Eight Illustrations and Map.

1887.

PREFACE TO SECOND EDITION.

THIS little volume is an abridgment of *The Life of Mahomet*, published by Messrs. Smith and Elder. It was prepared on behalf of the RELIGIOUS TRACT SOCIETY, with the view of giving, in small compass and easy form, the substance of the larger work. But it has been the Author's endeavour that nothing should be omitted essential to a fair understanding either of the Prophet's life, or of the Faith established by him.

The facts on which the narrative is based have been taken direct from the earliest Arabian authorities, of which an account is given in the larger work. At the same time full advantage has been taken of the standard biographies of *Weil* and *Sprenger*.

The present edition differs in no way from the first, excepting in occasional amendments, chiefly verbal, and in several illustrations drawn and engraved from Ali Bey, Burton, and a beautifully illustrated volume, *La Civilization des Arabes*, by Dr. Le Gustave de Bon.

W. M.

University of Edinburgh,
January 1887.

CONTENTS.

LIST OF ILLUSTRATIONS.

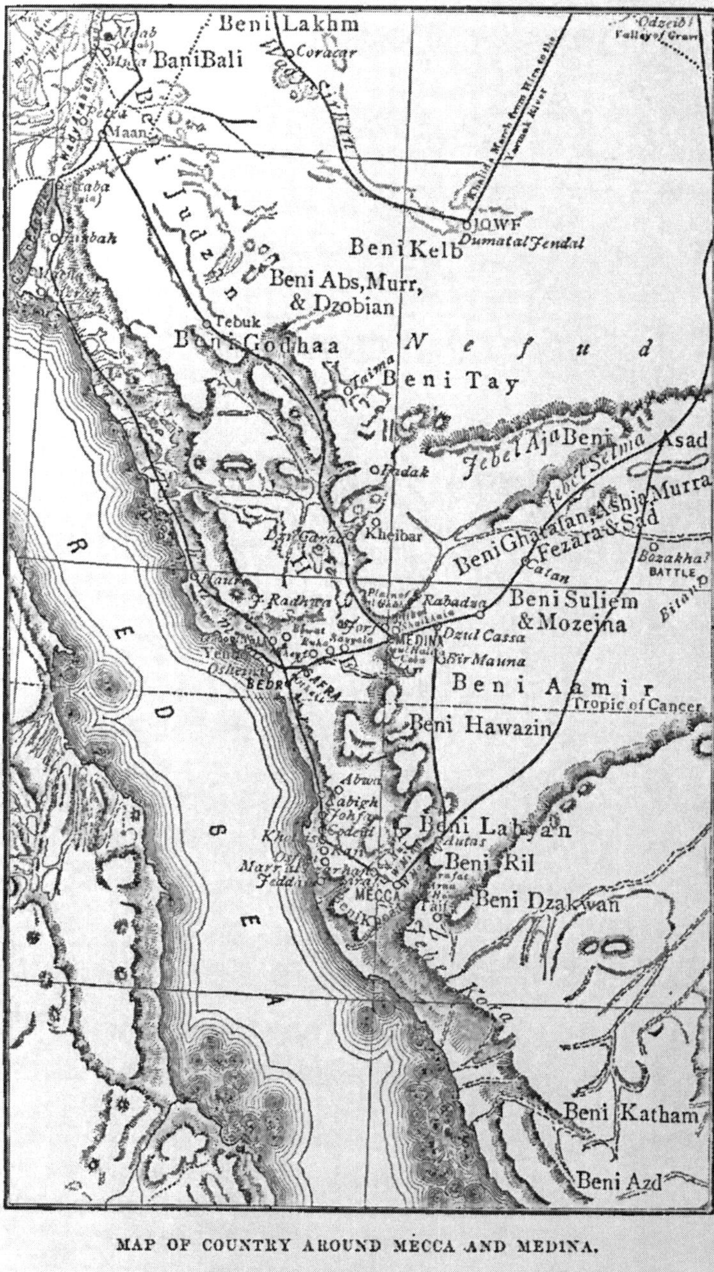

MAP OF COUNTRY AROUND MECCA AND MEDINA.

MAHOMET AND ISLAM.

CHAPTER I.

BIRTH AND CHILDHOOD.

Mecca, the Káaba, and the Coreish.

THE prophet of Arabia was born at Mecca in the year of our Lord 570. He sprang from the Coreish, a tribe that ruled over the city and neighbourhood. Close to Mecca stood the Káaba, an ancient temple of rude construction, which, with its idols and sacred surroundings, was the object of national worship, and the scene of an ever-recurring pilgrimage to which the Arabs flocked from the utmost bounds of the peninsula. As guardians of the Káaba and controllers of its worship, the Coreish were held in high regard by all Arabia. They were divided into several branches, and that to which the family of the prophet belonged was at this time in the ascendant.

The father of Mahomet.

The father of Mahomet was Abdallah, son of Abd al Muttălib, a leading citizen. His mother's name was Amĭna. Shortly after their marriage his father set out on a trading trip to Syria, with which country there was frequent communication by caravan. On his journey back he was taken ill at Medina, and died there. He left his widow a dwelling-house, five camels, and a slave-girl, Omm Ayman, who served in the household. The inheritance, though small, was, with the simple habits of the Arabs, a sign rather of prosperity than of want. Soon after Abdallah's death Amina gave birth to a son. She sent to tell Abd al Muttalib, who was glad, and carrying the infant to the Káaba, there gave thanks for its birth. The child was named *Muhammed,* "the Praised"; but in Europe it has been the usage to call him MAHOMET. Tradition surrounds his infant years with many tales, most of which are fond and marvellous. All that can be gleaned from these with tolerable confidence is given below.

Put out to nurse with a Bedouin tribe.

It was the custom for Coreishite mothers to give their infants out to nurse with some Bedouin tribe, gaining for them thus, instead of a sickly climate, the free and bracing desert air. After being nursed for some days by a slave-girl (to whom, as his foster-mother, Mahomet used to send gifts of raiment in token of regard), the orphan child was made over by his mother to Halîma, one of a party of the Beni Sad, who came to offer themselves as nurses, and was taken by her to their encampment. Two years were spent with this roving tribe, and then Halîma weaned the infant, and brought him back to Amina. Delighted with his healthy look, she said, "Take the child with thee back again, for much do I fear for him the unwholesome air of Mecca;" so she took him back. When two years more were ended, she appeared again, but this time disturbed in mind. Something like a fit had happened to the child, and, attributing it to the influence of an evil spirit, Halîma and her husband were anxious to be rid of the charge. She was persuaded to carry him back once more, and for another year she fondly tended him. But fresh symptoms returning, she finally restored him to his mother when five years of age.

Mahomet long after retained the grateful recollection of Halîma's care. In a year of drought, seeking help of him at Mecca, she received the present of a riding camel and a flock of sheep. At another visit he spread his mantle out for her to sit upon, and placed his hand in filial fondness on her bosom. Years passed, and in a campaign in which the Beni Sad were beaten, many prisoners of the tribe received their freedom, on reminding the prophet of his having been nursed among them. On the same occasion, a woman taken captive declared herself the daughter of Halîma and so his foster-sister. "See this mark," she said, "of the bite I got from thee, when once I carried thee on my hip." It was true; and he offered her the choice of a rich present, or of remaining in honour by him. She chose to return with the present to her people. It is possible that the fits to which the child was subject, may have had some connection with the ecstatic swoons of which mention will be made hereafter. But in other respects the desert life added robustness to his frame, and also force to his speech by fashioning it on one of the purest models of the Arabian tongue.

Grateful remembrance of Halîma.

The sixth year was spent with his mother at Mecca. At this time she planned a visit to Medina, where she longed to show the child to the relatives of his father's grandmother, who had come from thence. They rode on two camels, and Omm Ayman tended the little boy. Amina alighted at the

Visits Medina with his mother: ætat. 6.

house where her husband had died, and close by which he was buried. In after years, when Mahomet came to live in Medina, he recognized the spot. "Here," he said, "in this house, my mother lodged with me. There I used to sport with Aynasa, a little maid, and with my cousins chased the birds that settled on the roof. Here is my father's tomb, and in that very pond I learned to swim."

Death of his mother.

After sojourning a month at Medina, Amina set out on her return home in the same manner as she had gone. About half way she fell sick and died. The little orphan was carried back to Mecca by Omm Ayman, who, though still quite young, was a faithful nurse to the child, and continued to be his constant attendant. The early loss of his mother was deeply felt by Mahomet, who was old enough to understand an orphan's desolation. In a passage of the Coran, in which he touchingly recounts the mercies of the Lord, he says, "Did He not take thee up an orphan, and found a refuge for thee?" Once, on pilgrimage from Medina to Mecca, stopping at his mother's tomb by the way, he lifted up his voice and wept. When they asked him concerning it, he said, "This is the grave of my mother, which the Lord hath permitted me to see. I asked leave to pray for her salvation, but it was not granted. Then calling her to mind, the tender memory of my mother overcame me, and I wept."

Guardianship of Abd al Muttalib.

The guardianship of his orphan grandchild was undertaken by Abd al Muttalib, now fourscore years of age, and fondly he discharged the trust. The little boy would run up and take possession of the rug on which the aged patriarch reclined in the shade of the Káaba. When his sons chased the child away, Abd al Muttalib would interpose and say, "Let my little son alone," stroke him on the head, and listen to his prattle. At home, the child would ever and anon quit his nurse and run into his grandfather's room, even while he was asleep.

But the guardianship of Abd al Muttalib was not of long duration. In two years he died. The little Mahomet felt his loss bitterly, and as he followed the bier was seen to weep. The bereavement told the more, because the sons of Abd al Muttalib, unable to maintain the ancestral dignity, had to relinquish some of the offices of state which had been held by him, and so descended to a lower state of life. The rival branch, called Beni Omeyya, profited by the decline of the house of Hâshim (the father of Abd al Muttalib), and continued in the ascendant until the conquest of Mecca by Mahomet. Thus early arose the rivalry between the *Hâshimite* and *Omeyyad* dynasties, of which we hear so much in the history of Islam.

Death of Abd al Muttalib: ætat. 8.

To his son Abu Tâlib, Abd al Muttalib on his death-bed committed the orphan. Abu Tâlib undertook and faithfully fulfilled the obligation. He made the lad sleep by his bedside, and go forth with him whenever he walked abroad; and this tender treatment he continued till Mahomet emerged from the helplessness of childhood.

Mahomet taken charge of by his uncle, Abu Tâlib.

Notwithstanding his noble birth, Abu Tâlib was poor. To better his means he undertook a trading expedition to Syria. He would have left Mahomet, now twelve years of age, behind; but when the caravan was on the point of starting, the lad clung to his protector, and Abu Tâlib, moved by his

Journey to Syria: ætat. 12.

entreaty, took him with him. The journey stretched to Bostra, perhaps still further north. It lasted several months, and Mahomet had thus the opportunity of seeing the Christian people of Syria with their churches and their worship. However sunk in superstition, these must have stood out in strong contrast with the rude and barbarous rites of the Meccan valley, and furnished food for his inquiring and reflective mind.

CHAPTER II.

YOUTH OF MAHOMET—HIS MARRIAGE. ÆTAT. 12—35.

LITTLE is told us of the youth of Mahomet. He used to attend a fair held yearly at a spot three days' journey from Mecca, where, besides a busy barter, he witnessed the vain-glorious contests in poetry and rhetoric so characteristic of Arab manners. At this fair also he met Jews and Christians, and gained, no doubt, some acquaintance with their teaching. In after life he used to refer with satisfaction to his having there met Coss, the bishop of Najrân, and having heard at his lips "the preaching of the Catholic faith of Abraham."

Fair of Ocâtz.

Coss, bishop of Najrân.

For several years a war, arising out of a quarrel at this fair, raged between the Coreish and a neighbouring tribe. Mahomet was present at it, but though nearly twenty years of age, showed little love for arms. He busied himself in gathering up the arrows of the enemy and handing them to his uncles. One authority, indeed, assigns to him a more active part, but still without enthusiasm:—"I remember," he used to say, "being present with my uncles in the war: I shot arrows at the enemy, and do not regret it."

Mahomet takes part in a war near Mecca: ætat. 20.

In another matter the youthful Mahomet displayed a livelier interest. After the death of Abd al Muttalib, the civil power became so divided that no strong arm remained to enforce the right and redress the wrong. Acts of glaring tyranny suggested to certain leaders of the Coreish a league such as might secure justice for the helpless. A feast was held, many joined it, and swore "by the avenging Deity that they would take part with the oppressed so long as there was a drop of water in the ocean, see their claim fulfilled, or satisfy it themselves." The confederacy was a wholesome check upon misrule, and in later years Mahomet was wont to say of it, "I would not exchange for the choicest camel in all Arabia the memory of having shared in the oath to stand by the oppressed."

Joins in a confederacy to enforce justice.

At one time, like other lads of Mecca, he tended the flocks of his neighbours on the surrounding hills. He would refer to this in after days, and say that the occupation comported with his prophetic calling, even as it did with that of David and Moses. Passing by, in one of his campaigns, some shrubs with purple berries, he cried, "Pick me out the blackest ones, for they are sweet. Even such I used to gather, feeding the flocks in the valley of Mecca; and truly no prophet hath been raised up, but first he hath done the work of a shepherd." As he watched his flocks by night in the solitudes of the desert, the twinkling stars and bright constellations gliding silently across the sky, and the tempest with its forked lightning and thunder rolling along the mountains, would suggest to him the irresistible powers of Nature, the speech which day utters to day, and the knowledge which night shows unto night. Indeed, nothing is so remarkable as the faith

Employed in youth as a Shepherd.

reposed by Mahomet in the Deity as an ever-present and all-controlling agency. Throughout the Coran the lesson is constantly enforced by eloquent appeals to Providence, and to such scenes as at this time must have been ever before his eyes.

In his youth reserved and temperate.

Tradition credits Mahomet with a propriety of demeanour and purity of manners rare among the youth of Mecca. Engaged one night, we are told, in feeding his flock, he said to a comrade, "If thou wilt watch awhile, I will go into the city, and there divert myself even as youths are wont to divert themselves by night." But as he entered the town a marriage feast drew him aside, and he fell asleep. Another night, proceeding with the same design, he was arrested by heavenly music, and sitting down slept till morning. "After that," said Mahomet, "I no more sought after folly, even until I had attained unto the prophetic office." Without laying too much stress on these and such-like fond traditions, we may yet assume it to be altogether in keeping with the modest reserve of Mahomet, that he should have shrunk from the coarse licentiousness about him. In all his dealings he was fair and upright, and as he grew in years his honourable bearing won for him the title of *Al Ameen*, "the faithful."

Khadîja a rich widow, employs him on a trip to Syria: ætat. 25.

In course of time, Abu Tâlib, finding the charge of an increasing family press heavily upon him, suggested to Mahomet, already emerging into manhood, that he might do something towards earning a livelihood for himself. "See here," he said, "is a caravan about to start for Syria, and Khadîja, our cousin, hath need of men to take its charge. If thou wert to offer, she might accept thee." Mahomet agreeing, his uncle went to Khadîja,[1] and asked whether she would have him; "but," added he, "we hear that thou hast hired such a one for two camels, and we would not that our nephew should have less than four." To which she made answer, "Hadst thou asked it for one of another tribe, I would readily have granted thy request; how much more now that thou askest it for one near of kin!" So the matter was settled, and Mahomet set out on the same route for Bostra which he had travelled thirteen years before. He had thus the opportunity in mature life of again witnessing the worship and superstitions of the Syrian Christians, and of deepening the impressions of childhood regarding them. Khadîja's servant was in charge of the venture, but it devolved on Mahomet to conduct the barter. It was a task little congenial with the retiring life of Mahomet to drive bargains with the chaffering Syrians. But his natural shrewdness carried him well through the business, and he returned with the balance more than usually in his favour.

Mahomet reports his success to Khadîja.

As Mahomet retraced his steps, and was now close to Mecca, Khadîja's servant, won by his courtesy throughout the journey, persuaded him to go forward and announce his good fortune in person to his mistress. The widowed lady, surrounded by her maidens, sat upon the roof of her house watching for the caravan, and caught first sight of Mahomet coming on his camel. At her bidding he ascended, reported the prosperous issue of the journey, and made mention of the various things which he had purchased for her. She was charmed with the success, but still more with the modest and noble bearing, of her youthful agent.

[1] Pronounce *Khadeeja.*

Khadîja was now forty years of age. She had been twice married, and had borne a daughter and two sons. Courted by many as comely, rich, and nobly born, she preferred an independent widowhood. But now, despite the difference of age, her heart was touched. For several days she endeavoured to stifle the passion, but without success. At last she sent her sister to make overtures to Mahomet. Sounding cautiously, this lady asked what it might be that hindered him from marrying. "I have nothing in my hands," he said, "wherewith I might marry." "But if haply thou wert called to espouse a well-favoured and noble lady, who could keep thee in comfort, wouldest thou not have her?" "And who," replied Mahomet, startled at the idea, "might that be?" "None other," she answered, "but my sister Khadîja." "And how might I attain unto her?" "Leave that to me, if thou wilt have her." At once he answered, "I am ready." The sister departed and told Khadîja.

Khadîja conceives a passion for Mahomet.

But the lady's father was a churl. Dreading his refusal, Khadîja prepared for him a feast, and when he had well drunk and was merry, they slaughtered a cow, and casting over the guests wedding raiment and perfumes, completed thus the marriage ceremony. Recovering from his debauch, the old man asked what all this meant,—the feast, the saffron garments, the perfumes, and the slaughtered cow? "The marriage dress," they said, "was cast over thee by Mahomet, thine own son-in-law." Thereupon he fell into a rage, and swore that he would never disgrace his daughter, courted by the chief men of the Coreish, by throwing her away on that poor youth. Weapons were drawn, and blood might have been shed.

Mahomet marries Khadîja: ætat. 25.

But at the last he was pacified by the assurance of the bridegroom's friends that the alliance, unsought by them, was none other than his own daughter's act.

His married life.

Notwithstanding this stormy opening and the disparity of years (for Mahomet was now but five-and-twenty, and she near forty [1]), the marriage proved a happy and not unfruitful one. Khadîja continued as before to superintend her household, and Mahomet, now free to pursue his meditations, made her the repository of the doubts and anxieties which began to agitate his soul. She bore him two sons and four daughters. The latter survived, but the boys died in infancy. The eldest son was called Câsim; and hence, after Arab wont, the prophet was surnamed Abul Câsim, that is, Câsim's father. In later years, Mahomet used to speak of this happy period in terms so warm and loving, that Ayesha, the young and favourite wife of his declining years, declared herself more jealous of Khadîja, whom she had never seen, than of all her rival "Sisters."

Mahomet described.

Mahomet was somewhat above middle height. His figure was spare, but carrying presence with it; the chest broad and open, the frame large, and joints well knit together. His neck was long and well moulded; his head massive, with a forehead broad and noble. Thick black hair, slightly curling, hung over his ears. The eyes were large, black, and piercing, fringed with long dark eyelashes; eyebrows arched and joined; cheeks thin and ruddy; nose high and aquiline, fine, and at the end attenuated. A long and bushy beard rested on his breast. His features

[1] Forty *lunar* years would be something under thirty-nine, by solar computation.

and expression were handsome, but pensive, and with something also of the sensuous.

His character.

Though the subject of strong passions, these rarely appeared on the surface. When excited, the vein would swell across his ample forehead. His eye, often bloodshot, was restless. The stranger looked with awe on his commanding mien; but this, on closer intimacy, gave place to confidence and regard. Decision marked his every movement; he turned towards you, not partially, but with the whole body. Taciturn and reserved, he still was singularly courteous. His speech was pregnant and laconic, often humorous and pungent. He would enter with zest into the diversion of the moment, and at times laugh immoderately. But in general he listened rather than spoke. Kind and faithful to his followers, he was remarkable for his many close and lasting friendships. Generous and large-hearted in public life, he knew how to gain over the disaffected by well-timed grace and gifts such as the Arab loved. But towards his enemies, especially in later years, he too often exhibited a vindictive and unrelenting hatred, although he rarely pursued the foe tendering a timely submission.

Khadîja's faith in Mahomet.

Such was Mahomet, as we learn from the descriptions given of him after he had come to power. At the present period there was little promise of future greatness. But behind the quiet exterior there lay a will and purpose destined to bow the heart of Arabia to himself as the heart of one man. This, Khadîja was the first to perceive. With implicit trust, she surrendered her faith in things divine as well as human into his hands.

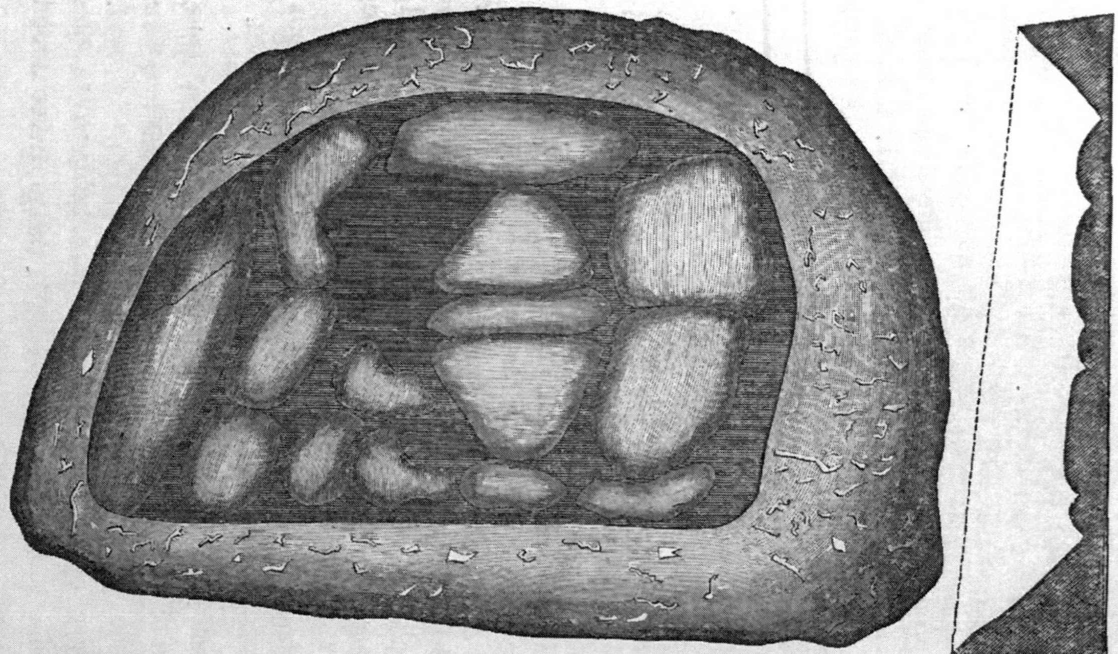

FRONT AND SIDE VIEWS OF THE BLACK STONE. (TAKEN FROM ALI BEY'S TRAVELS.) HALF ACTUAL SIZE.

CHAPTER III.

REBUILDING OF THE KÁABA—ALY AND ZEID—SPIRITUAL ASPIRATIONS—THE FOUR ENQUIRERS.

The Káaba and the rites of pilgrimage.

Ten years after his marriage, Mahomet was present at the rebuilding of the Káaba. The edifice, a plain square house,[1] was of great antiquity. Fable ascribes its foundation to Abraham. The well hard by is called the Well of Hagar; for this is the spot, according to the fond tradition, on which the disconsolate mother cast her thirsty child, while in distress she paced rapidly to and fro between the neighbouring eminences of Safa and Merwa in search of water; when suddenly the fountain Zem-zem bubbled up at the feet of the wailing Ishmael. In front of the temple was the great image of Hobal, the tutelary god of Mecca; other idols were ranged around, and at a respectful distance stood the habitations of the Coreish. The great pilgrimage was held annually in one of the three months during which war was suspended. The devotees assembled from all quarters and in vast numbers at Mecca. They kissed the Black Stone (perhaps an aerolite) built into a corner of the "house

[1] Káaba means a square or cube, whence probably the name. It was also called *Beitullah*, the "house of God."

of God," and drank of the sacred well. Two or three days more were spent in visiting Mount Arafat, a little hill twelve miles up the valley. Victims were slain at Minâ, half way on the return to Mecca. And so ended the "Greater Pilgrimage." That part of the worship limited to the Káaba and its immediate pre-

THE KÁABA, AS IT NOW STANDS, SHOWING THE CURTAIN FESTOONED AT PILGRIMAGE, AND THE BLACK STONE IN POSITION (*a*).[1]

cincts could be performed at any period of the year, and was called the "Lesser Pilgrimage."

The Káaba having been injured by a flood, had now

[1] *b*, curtain of door suspended from roof for show; *c*, door; *d*, golden spout for rain. Both pictures are from Ali Bey's Travels.

fallen into disrepair. Despite the dread of vengeance at the sacrilege, it had to be pulled down, and then built up again from the foundation. As the walls rose, a quarrel broke out among the leading families as to which should deposit the Black Stone in its place. They had nearly come to blows, when one proposed that the first citizen seen approaching

Káaba rebuilt: ætat. 35.

THE KÁABA, AS IT NOW STANDS, SHOWING THE CURTAIN CUT AND ADJUSTED.

the temple should arbitrate between them. It was no sooner agreed upon than Mahomet came in sight. "Lo, it is the Faithful one!" they cried, "we are content." Spreading his mantle on the ground, he bade them place the stone upon it. "Now," said he, addressing the contending families, "let a chief man from each of you seize a corner of this mantle, and raise the stone." When it had reached the proper height, Mahomet with his own hand guided it home. The building was then completed. It was roofed in with rafters, the wreck of a Greek ship cast ashore at Jedda, whose captain aided in the work of reconstruction. A black curtain was then thrown over the edifice, hanging down (as a similar curtain still hangs) like a veil all round.[1]

Mahomet adopts Aly and Zeid.

About this time, to make up for the loss of his own infant son, as well as to lighten the burdens of the father, Mahomet adopted his cousin Aly, son of Abu Tâlib. The lad was now but five or six years of age; and a close attachment prevailed between them ever after. Soon after, he admitted Zeid, son of Hâritha, to a like relation and a life-long friendship. This was a youth twenty years of age, who, when a child, having been seized by brigands and sold into captivity, was now possessed by Khadîja. Short,

[1] This is the so-called "Carpet" sent with sacred honours from Cairo at the yearly pilgrimage to Mecca. The wood-cut from Ali Bey shows how in the present day it hangs from the roof, and "clothes" the building as far down as the door. As it now stands, the Káaba, built of fine grey granite slabs, is some 40 feet in height, 45 to 50 long, and 35 to 40 broad. The sill of the doorway is 7 feet from the ground; and as there is no stair to it, the interior—an empty Hall—can be entered only by a wooden staircase rolled up to the spot. The Black Stone, an irregular oval, 7 inches in diameter, stands 4 or 5 feet from the ground, let in at the S.E. corner. Burkhardt tells us it is "a reddish-brown, approaching to black;"—"worn to its present surface by the millions of touches and kisses it has received." Ali Bey, whose picture of it is given above (p. 24), describes it as "a fragment of volcanic basalt, sprinkled throughout its circumference with small pointed crystals varied with red feldspath, upon a dark black ground like coal, except one of its protuberances, which is a little reddish. The continual kisses and touchings of the faithful have worn the surface uneven, so that it now has a muscular appearance. It has nearly 15 muscles and one deep hollow."

dark, and ill-favoured, he was active and useful in his mistress's service. Mahomet conceived a strong affection for him, and, to gratify her husband, Khadîja made a present to him of the slave. Zeid's father, who had searched long in vain, at last got tidings of him from a party who had been on pilgrimage to Mecca. Setting out thither, he offered Mahomet a large sum in ransom of his son; but Zeid chose rather to stay on with his master. "I will not leave thee," he said; "thou art more than father and mother to me." Mahomet upon this, to seal the transaction, carried him to the Black Stone of the Káaba, and there before all said, "Bear ye witness, Zeid is my son; he is mine heir, and I am his." The father went away contented; and thenceforward the slave, now freed, was known as "Zeid the son of Mahomet." He married the nurse Omm Ayman, who, though double his age (and for the unequal yoke the prophet gave promise of a special reward in paradise), bore him a son, Osâma, in after years a commander of renown.

Acquaintance with Jews and Christians.

The parents of Zeid belonged to a people among whom Christianity prevailed; and, though torn from them in early life, he no doubt retained, and was able to impart to his adopted father, some impression of the ancestral faith. Among the kinsmen of Khadîja, too, there were persons who knew something of the tenets, if they did not observe the precepts, of the gospel. A cousin of that lady, having been baptized at the Byzantine court, sought by aid of an imperial rescript to seize the government of Mecca, but failing in the attempt, retired to the Christian court of Bostra. Another cousin, the aged Waraca, is spoken of as having embraced Christianity, and even translated portions of the Jewish and Christian Scriptures into Arabic. Indeed, a spirit of inquiry appears to have been fermenting throughout Arabia at this time; for we are told of *Four Enquirers*, who were in search of what they called "the Catholic faith of Abraham." One of these, named Zeid, condemned the idolatry of the Káaba, reprobated female infanticide, and foretold Mahomet (so the legend runs) as the prophet that was to come. Jewish and Christian slaves were frequently to be met with at Mecca, and Jewish tribes had long been settled in Medina and its neighbourhood, with whom the Coreish were intimate. From all these sources Mahomet was in a position to learn something of the Scriptures, both of the Old Testament and the New.

The Four Enquirers.

The daughters of Mahomet were now growing up around him. The eldest was early married to a nephew of his wife, and two others to sons of his uncle Abu Lahab. Mahomet himself lived in comfort, but his mind became ill at ease. He was already forty years of age, when, prompted perhaps by teaching from the sources just described, or spontaneously from within, grave doubts arose. The debasement of his people grew a heavy burden, and his soul was troubled with questionings as to what might be the true religion. Oppressed thus, he oft retired to meditate. His favourite resort was a cave on the declivities of Mount Hirâ, two or three miles from Mecca. "The country before us," says a traveller describing the retreat, "had a dreary aspect, not a single green spot being visible; barren black and grey hills and white sandy valleys were the only objects in sight,"—meet surroundings for Mahomet's perplexed spirit.

Spiritual anxiety.

Frequents cave on Mount Hirâ.

Thither he would stroll, and remain away for days together, his faithful wife joining him at times. Close by was the tomb of the "Enquirer" Zeid, who, after a lifetime spent in like anxieties, had now reached the land of certainty. Might he not attain the same assurance, even this side the gates of death?

The following chapter will explain in what these reveries found their issue.

CHAPTER IV.

FIRST DREAMS OF INSPIRATION. ÆTAT. 40—43.

Poetical fragments and rhapsodies.

LIGHT struggled with the darkness in the soul of Mahomet. Gradually certain grand verities took clear and definite shape before him:—God, the sole Creator, Ruler and Judge of men and angels; the hopeless wretchedness of men sunk in heathenism and idolatry; heaven and hell; the resurrection, judgment, and recompense of good and evil in the world to come. The conflict waging within found vent in such impassioned fragments as these:—

Sura c.

I swear by the rushing panting steeds!
Striking fire with flashing hoof,
Scouring the land at early morn;
And darkening it with dust,
As they overwhelm the foe!
Verily Man is to his Lord ungrateful,
Verily he is keen after this world's good.
Ah! witteth he not that when what is in the graves shall be scattered,
And that which is in men's breasts shall be revealed;—
Verily the Lord shall in that day be informed thereof.

And again:—

Sura xcv.

I swear by the Fig-tree and the Olive!
By Mount Sinai, and by this land secure!

Verily WE created man of the choicest fabric,
Then WE made him the vilest of the vile,
  Excepting such as believe and work righteousness;
  Unto them shall be given a reward that fadeth not away.
Then, after this what shall make thee deny the Day of reckoning?
  What! is not God the most just of Judges?

And yet another specimen:—

  Woe unto all backbiters and defamers; Sura civ.
  To him that heapeth up riches and numbereth the same!
He thinketh that his wealth shall remain with him for ever.
  Nay, verily! he shall be cast into the Crushing Fire.
And what shall make thee know what is the Crushing Fire?
  It is the kindled Fire of God which mounteth above the hearts,
Verily it shall mount above them as a curtain stretched over lofty columns.

Mental distress and ecstasies.

These wild and incoherent rhapsodies are couched in words of rare beauty and force, with such flow and rhythm as the Arab loves, and which his noble tongue gives the freest scope to. The oracle, it will be observed, purports to come direct from the Deity, speaking always as "We" (which if not expressed is to be understood,) and so addressed to Mahomet as "Thou." The conviction, however, of being inspired of God was not reached by Mahomet till after a protracted trial of mental throes. At times, we are told, the distress was so great as even to suggest escape by suicide. There were periods at which the excitement took the shape of a trance or vision. Of these we know but little. Some early Christian writers have described them as epileptic seizures, and have connected them with the symptoms noticed in his childhood. Such swoons or reveries are said sometimes to have preceded "the descent of inspiration," even in later life. What the nature of these ecstasies was it is difficult to conjecture. It will suffice to let tradition speak for itself, and leave the reader to draw his own conclusion. Premising that on a mysterious subject like this, imagination must have had the fullest play in the process of oral transmission, I give the narrative from the pen of the earliest biographers;—

"First beginnings of inspiration," as handed down by tradition.

"The first beginnings of Mahomet's inspiration," we are told, "were *real visions*. Every vision that he saw was clear as the morning dawn. These again provoked the love of solitude. He would repair to Mount Hirâ, and there pass whole days and nights. Then, drawn by affection for Khadîja, he would return to his home. This went on till the truth burst upon him in the cave at Hirâ. It happened on this wise. Wandering in the hills thereabouts, an angel from the sky cried, '*O Mahomet, I am Gabriel!*' He was terrified, for as often as he raised his head, there was the apparition of the angel. He hurried home to tell his wife. 'Oh, Khadîja,' he said, 'I have never abhorred anything as I do these idols and soothsayers; and now verily I fear lest I should become a soothsayer myself.' 'Never,' replied his faithful wife; 'the Lord will never suffer it thus to be,'—and she went on to speak of his many virtues, upon which she founded the assurance. Then she repaired to her cousin Waraca, and told him all. 'By the Lord,' cried the aged man, 'he speaketh truth! Doubtless it is the beginning of prophecy, and there shall come upon him the *Great Nomos* (the Law), like as it came upon Moses. Wherefore charge him that he think not aught but hopeful thoughts within his breast. If he be raised up a prophet while I am yet alive, surely I will stand by him.'

The first "Revelation."

"Now on the night that the Lord was minded to be gracious unto him, Gabriel appeared to Mahomet in the cave, and holding a writing up before him, said, '*Read.*' He answered, 'I cannot.' Whereupon the angel did so tightly gripe him that he thought his last moment was come. '*Read!*' cried Gabriel the second time; and thereupon, but only to escape the agony, Mahomet said, 'What shall I read?' Gabriel then went on—

Read! in the name of thy Lord that created,—
Sura xcvi. Created man from congealed blood.

Read! for thy Lord is most gracious;
It is He that hath taught to write with the pen,
Hath taught man that which he knoweth not;
Nay, verily, for man is rebellious
When he seeth himself becoming rich;—

[And so on with what is now the xcvi. Sura (or chapter) of the Coran.] When he had ended, the angel departed. 'And the words,' said Mahomet, 'were as though they had been graven into my heart.' After this he waited long,—it may have been months, some think a year, or even two years,—and no angel came. He grew downcast, and fearing possession of devils, had thoughts of destroying himself. Wandering thus and seeking with that object for some precipice, he was suddenly arrested by Gabriel seated on a throne in the sky, and calling, '*O Mahomet, thou art the Prophet of the Lord, and I am Gabriel.*' So he turned from what he had been minded to do, and went to his home.

Second appearance of Gabriel.

"At another time, terrified by rushing thoughts, he besought Khadîja to cover him over, and as he lay trembling the word came to arise and preach:—

The command to preach.

Sura lxxiv.

O thou that art covered,
Arise and preach,
And magnify thy Lord,
And purify thy garments,
And depart from all uncleanness,
And show not favour seeking for thine own aggrandisement;—

[And so on with what is now the lxxiv. Sura.]

"Thus the Lord comforted His prophet and strengthened his heart. And thereafter revelations began to follow one upon another with frequency.

"At the moment of inspiration (so the tradition runs) anxiety pressed upon the prophet, and his countenance became troubled. Sweat dropped from his forehead, and he would fall to the ground as in a trance. 'Inspiration,' he would say, 'cometh to me in one of two ways. At times Gabriel speaketh the word unto me as one man speaketh to another, and this is easy. At other times it is like the ringing of a bell, it penetrateth my heart, and rendeth me; and this it is which afflicteth me the most.' In later life he would point to his grey hairs, and say that they were the withering effect of the earlier terrific Suras."

The descent of inspiration.

How far Mahomet was sincere in the belief of his own inspiration.

The ground all round, as I have said, would naturally be prolific in growth of the marvellous; yet some kind of reverie or trance, both now and in later days, there must sometimes have been whereon such traditions were founded. "Revelations" of the nature here described, all shaped as messages or commands direct from God, continued to "descend" upon the prophet throughout his life, and as such were termed the *Corân*, or Word of God.[1] As his life advanced these began to lose the glow and fervour of the first rhapsodies. Ever and anon, indeed, even to the end, we meet with passages—those especially on the Being and Providence of God—grand, impassioned, and kindling with the early fire; but the ordinary style becomes tame and vapid. Moreover, when Mahomet attained to temporal power, the "revelation" was used as the means of not only reaching secular ends, but even of ministering to his lower instincts. While, therefore, there is no reason to question the sincerity of Mahomet in the earlier period of his career, the same cannot be said, or at the least it must be said in a very different sense, in respect of his later years. It will be for the reader himself to judge, from the materials placed before him, when and to what extent, consciously or unconsciously, self-deception obscured the spiritual vista;—whether, in fact, the eye being no longer single, "the whole body did not become full of darkness."

[1] *Corân;* meaning that which is "read" or "recited."

CHAPTER V.

EARLY MINISTRY AND CONVERTS—PERSECUTION—FLIGHT TO ABYSSINIA. ÆTAT. 44—47.

So soon as Mahomet had emerged from his doubts and difficulties into what he conceived to be the light of a Divine revelation, he began to canvas for adherents from amongst his friends and relatives. The first disciples were of his own household —Khadîja, Zeid, Omm Ayman, Aly, and some others. "And Khadîja believed" (thus runs the simple tradition), "and attested the truth of that which came upon her husband from above. For so the Lord was minded to lighten the burden of His servant; he heard nothing that grieved him in being rejected by his people, but he had recourse unto her, and she comforted and strengthened him."

First converts from his own household.

While as yet there was no public ministry, and the teaching of Mahomet was still in private, a group of forty or fifty converts rallied round him, all animated by devotion to his person and belief in God as his guide and inspirer. These were chiefly from amongst the young. But there was one of mature age, the bosom friend of Mahomet, called Abu Bekr, who was just three years younger than he. Mild and tender-hearted, he was yet shrewd and able. Abu Bekr early

Other disciples.

cast in his lot with the prophet, and through all the changing scenes of his life to the end was to him a pillar of strength. His daughter Ayesha (destined while yet a girl to be the bride of Mahomet) "could not remember the time when both her father and mother were not believers, and when the prophet did not visit their house morning and evening." And Mahomet used to say of him, "I never invited any one to the faith who did not at the first show hesitation and perplexity, saving only Abu Bekr, who, when I had propounded Islam unto him, tarried not, neither was perplexed." He was at this time a prosperous merchant, and he devoted his fortune to the purchase and freeing of such converted slaves as were persecuted by their unbelieving masters.

Public ministry. Having at last (as he conceived) the commission to "arise and preach," Mahomet began publicly to exercise his ministry. The teaching, though as yet elementary, was decisive and dogmatic. He called the new way *Islâm*, or "surrender" of the will to God. He was himself a prophet, like those of olden times, but sent specially to the Arabs, because no revelation had heretofore been made to them, none at the least which was embodied in their mother tongue. Idols were an abomination. The Deity, unapproachable in his ineffable Unity, was infinitely exalted above the vain conceits men had imagined concerning him. To regard any creatures as "partners" of the Almighty, or as "associated" with him, was intolerable infidelity. The Arabs were summoned to return to this the grand Catholic faith, which underlay all previous dispensations,—the "faith of Abraham," their great progenitor. They were warned of the resurrection, of the judgment to come, and of the retribution of good and evil in heaven and hell. Such was the simple doctrine urged by Mahomet with solemn earnestness as the Messenger of God.

Persecution.

At first his teaching was treated as that of a harmless enthusiast. The Coreish heard him with curious disdain. As he passed, they would point slightingly after him, saying, "There goeth the man of the children of Muttalib to speak to the people about the heavens." But no sooner did he denounce their idols, and tell them that their ancestors were all hopelessly lost, than they became angry. They began then to treat him with contumely, and his followers with harshness. Their pride was hurt; for the men of Mecca were vain of the Káaba, and conservative of its worship. They could not understand the freedom of conscience which at this time was preached by Mahomet. The same spirit was aroused as caused the multitude of old to shout, "Great is Diana of the Ephesians." The worship of the Káaba was in danger to be set at nought, and so the new doctrine must be crushed. By degrees the persecution grew hot. The free converts for the most part escaped serious injury; those at least whose families made it a point of tribal honour to secure their personal safety.

Suffering of converted slaves.

But there was no such sentiment to protect the slaves, and such others as did not belong to some one of the more powerful households. These were exposed to much suffering. They were placed in confinement; they were taken forth under a burning sun and cast upon the scorching gravel in the valley without the city. If, when tormented thus, they denied Mahomet, and acknowledged the idols, they were at once refreshed with draughts of water and carried to their homes. Belâl, a tall, dark, gaunt negro, alone remained firm. They could draw from him in his anguish but the cry, "One! one (God) alone!" It was at such a time that Abu Bekr passed by and ransomed the faithful confessor. For the rest Mahomet showed much sympathy. One approached him sobbing. "They would not let me go," he said, "until I had reviled thee and spoken well of their gods." "But how is it with thy heart?" "Steadfast," he replied. "Then," answered Mahomet, "if they repeat their cruelties, do thou repeat thy words." And a special dispensation is declared in the Coran for those forced thus to deny their faith.

Fifteen converts fly for refuge to Abyssinia: ætat. 47.

Mahomet himself was safe. His uncle Abu Tâlib, though not himself a believer, remained faithful in his guardianship. But opposition increased daily. The doctrine of the Resurrection was scouted. "What!" cried the Coreish; "when we have died and become dust and dry bones, shall we be raised up to life again?" The threats of a judgment to come were laughed to scorn. The terrors of hell, with its "scorching blasts and scalding water," were as ineffectual as the charms of paradise, with its green shades and voluptuous Houris. The grand appeals which the prophet made to the power, the providence, and the vengeance of the Almighty, fell on listless ears. His declamations against their idols excited the wrath of the citizens, and the growing number of his followers stirred their alarm and aggravated their hatred. At last things came to such a pass, that Mahomet desired those who were able, to seek an asylum elsewhere. "Yonder," he said, pointing to the west, "is a land of righteousness. Depart thither until the Lord shall open out for us a way." So a band of fifteen took shipping, crossed the Red Sea, and found a refuge in Abyssinia, where they were hospitably entertained by the Negus,[1] or Christian king. Among these was Rockeya, the prophet's daughter, and her husband Othmân, one of the earliest converts. This is called the first *Hegira*,[2] or "flight." It took place in the fifth year of the ministry of Mahomet.

[1] In Arabic *Najâshy*. The King of Abyssinia is still so called, or *Negoosa*, as in Hewitt's recent treaty.

[2] Pronounced with the *i* short.

CHAPTER VI.

THE LAPSE—SECOND FLIGHT TO ABYSSINIA—CONVERSION OF OMAR AND HAMZA—THE BAN. ÆTAT. 45—49. A.D. 615—619.

Return of the Refugees.

THE refugees were gone hardly three months when they reappeared at Mecca. They had been induced to return by the rumour reaching Abyssinia that Mecca was converted to Islam. There had, indeed, been a temporary reunion. The story is strange and obscure, but the leading facts are beyond question.

Mahomet's lapse.

It was Mahomet himself who had made a compromise with his fellow-citizens. In an incautious moment (so we are told), he agreed to regard their idols as representatives of the Deity.

> See ye not *Lât* and *Ozza*,
> And *Manât* the third besides?

Such is a verse of the Coran, referring to the three tutelary gods of Mecca. To this, in the hearing of the assembled worshippers, Mahomet added, "*These are the exalted goddesses whose intercession with the Deity is to be sought.* . . . Wherefore bow ye down and worship before Him." Then spake the people: "Now know we that it is the Lord alone which killeth and maketh alive, which giveth life and taketh it away. As for these our goddesses, they do but intercede with Him.

Wherefore, as thou hast given to them a place, we are content." And they bowed themselves down and worshipped. But Mahomet soon repented of what he had done. He was ill at ease and grieved in his heart. And so, after a time, he recalled the concession, and gave forth the passage, as we now find it in the Coran, where the three goddesses are named as above, but with the addition of these two verses:—

Compromise recalled and persecution renewed.

> What! shall there be male progeny unto you and female unto Him? (Sura liii.)
> That were indeed an unjust partition.[1]
> These are nought but names which ye and your fathers have invented.

The Coreish were wroth. They had been affronted and befooled. And so the persecution was resumed more bitterly than ever.

Such is the story as we gather from tradition. Some authorities, indeed, ignore it altogether; but something of the kind, to bring back the emigrants from Abyssinia, must certainly have taken place. Mahomet himself, once recovered, went on preaching as before. His utterances breathe ever more and more iconoclastic zeal. The heavenly oracle warns him against tampering with inspiration, from a desire to deal gently with his people, or being tempted by their pomp and numbers to quit the narrow path. The lapse itself is thus referred to:—

Mahomet's stern denunciation of idolatry.

> Truly they were near tempting thee away from that which WE revealed unto thee, to fabricate in respect of Us a diverse Revelation, and then they would have taken thee for their friend.
> If it had not been that WE established thee, verily they were near inclining unto thee a little;

---

[1] *Female* progeny being looked down upon in Arabia.

Then verily WE had caused thee to taste the punishment of life and the punishment of death.
And then thou hadst not found against Us any helper. Sura xvii.

Thenceforward he never wavered in his stern denunciation of polytheism. "Your idols are idleness and vanity," he would say to his fellow-citizens:—

They have not any power, no, not over the husk of a date.
If ye call upon them, they hear not your calling.
If they heard, neither would they answer you: Sura xxxv.
And in the Day of Judgment they will disown your worship.

Second flight to Abyssinia.

By the time that the returning refugees reached Mecca, the compromise was not only a thing of the past, but persecution had set in with redoubled violence. By the advice of Mahomet they again fled to Abyssinia. The account they sent back to Mecca of their reception was so favourable, that the party was recruited from time to time by fresh accessions from Mecca, till there was gathered a band of as many as a hundred Moslems at the court of the Christian Negus. The Coreish took alarm, and sent a deputation demanding their surrender; but the King refused, and ever after remained their firm protector. Islam was as yet the coadjutor, rather than the rival, of Christianity; and, in point of fact, some of the refugees while in Abyssinia themselves embraced the faith of the gospel.

Abu Tâlib braves the Coreish and stands by Mahomet.

Mahomet was now himself not free from peril. The elders of the Coreish repaired angrily to Abu Tâlib. "This nephew of thine," they cried, "hath said opprobrious things of our gods, hath upbraided us as fools, and hath spoken of our forefathers as hopelessly lost. Now, then, either avenge us of our adversary, or leave him, that we may take satisfaction for ourselves." Abu Tâlib put them off with courteous words; but the breach widened daily. They came again, and reiterated their demand more roughly. "We cannot bear it any longer," they said. "Wherefore, do thou hold him back from us, or else thyself take part with him, that the matter may be decided between us." Troubled in spirit, he called his nephew to him, and explaining the strait into which they had driven him, continued earnestly, "Now, therefore, save thyself and me also, and cast not on me a burden heavier than I can bear." Mahomet made answer, "Oh, my uncle, if they should place the sun on my right hand and the moon on my left to turn me aside, I will not desist until that the Lord make manifest my cause, or else I perish in the struggle." He turned to go. But the thought of desertion by his kind protector overcame him, and he burst into tears. The aged chief was moved too. "Son of my brother," he cried, "come back. And now depart in peace, and say whatsoever thou wilt; for, by the Lord of the Káaba, I will not in any wise give thee up for ever." And so things went on again for a time. The life of Mahomet was safe under the guardianship of his noble relative, though he had often to bear humiliation and indignity at the hands of his powerful enemies.

Conversion of Hamza and Omar.

About this time his cause was strengthened unexpectedly by the conversion of two citizens of note, Hamza son of Abd al Muttalib's old age, and Omar. On a certain occasion, Hamza, who was little older than his nephew the prophet, was roused, on hearing him violently abused, to take his part; and having once done so, he cast in his lot heart and soul with the new faith. The conversion of Omar was equally sudden, and the tale even more romantic. He belonged to another branch of the Coreish, and was yet in the pride of early manhood. Happening unexpectedly to enter the house of his sister, he found her, to his surprise, engaged with her husband in reading a chapter of the new revelation. He fell into a passion, and in the scuffle that ensued wounded her face. Seeing blood flow, he was softened, and asked to see the roll. As he deciphered it word by word, he exclaimed, "How excellent is this discourse, and gracious! Lead me to Mahomet, that I may declare my conversion unto him." So they took him to the house where the prophet secretly, for fear of the Coreish, received his disciples, and knocked. The inmates, seeing Omar, were alarmed; but Mahomet bade them to let him in, and catching hold of the stranger's sword-belt, said, "How long, O Omar, wilt thou not cease from persecuting? even until the Lord send some calamity upon thee!" Omar made answer, "Verily I testify that thou art the prophet of God." Filled with delight, Mahomet cried aloud, "*Allah Akbar!* Great is the Lord!"

The Coreish alarmed;

The adhesion of two such men was a real triumph to the cause. Of Omar especially the Coreish stood in dread. Commanding in stature, powerful and brave, he was also hot-tempered and impetuous. From a cause of anxiety and alarm to Mahomet, he now was suddenly converted into a tower of strength. This produced a change which soon was manifest in the increasing boldness of the converts. The claims of religion began to over-ride the bonds of kinship, and members of the same family might be seen ranged on either side. The disciples emerged from their secret resorts. Conscious of strength, they assembled in knots around the Káaba, and there performed their simple worship openly. Dread fell on the Coreish. Their embassy had returned from Abyssinia crestfallen. Checked as they were at every turn, what were they now to do? Accordingly they struck out a new device. Mahomet they saw supported not only by his own disciples, but also, with the exception of Abu Lahab, by his relatives the children of Hâshim, who held themselves bound, whether converted or not, to keep their kinsman safe. The rest of the Coreish now bound themselves in a confederacy together. The Beni Hâshim were cut off from their society and excommunicated. All dealings of any kind whatever were forbidden. Marriage ceased between them; even buying and selling was proscribed. The ban was committed to writing, sealed, and, to give it greater sanctity, hung up in the Káaba.

Enter into a confederacy against the Beni Hâshim;

Unable to withstand this hostile demonstration, the Beni Hâshim withdrew into the "Quarter" of Abu Tâlib. This quarter formed a defile separated from the rest of the city by projecting rocks of the overhanging hill, and was approached only by a narrow alley closed by a gateway. Here, though safe from insult, they were cut off from the supplies of daily life, and often suffered the extremities of want. Only at the yearly pilgrimage,—season of universal amnesty,—they were free to issue forth. Of these occasions Mahomet made good use. He preached to the pilgrims who congregated at Mecca and the neighbouring fairs, but with small effect. His steps were dogged by his uncle, Abu Lahab, who would say, "Believe him not; he is a lying renegade;" and the listeners would make answer to his

Who retire into the quarter of Abu Tâlib.

Mahomet preaches at seasons of pilgrimage.

call, "Thine own people should know thee best; why is it that they have cast thee off?" And so day after day he returned to his home dispirited and grieved.

Bitter relations with Abu Lahab.

The embittered relations between Abu Lahab and his nephew, notwithstanding that two of his sons had married daughters of Mahomet, may be gathered from a memorable passage in the Coran. The prophet, we are told, called his relatives together to hear his message. When he had delivered it, "Blast the fellow!" cried Abu Lahab; "is that all that he hath called us for together?" To chide the blasphemer, and also to curse his wife, who had strewn thorns in his path, this drastic Sura, containing a savage play upon the name,[1] was promulgated:—

> Blasted be the hands of Abu Lahab! and let himself be blasted!
> His riches shall not profit him, nor that which he hath gained.
> He shall be cast into the broiling *Flame;*
> His wife also, laden with fuel,
> A halter of palm-coir round her neck. (Sura cxi.)

The Beni Hâshim for three years under the ban: ætat. 49—51.

It was in the seventh year of the ministry of Mahomet that the children of Hâshim entered the Quarter of Abu Tâlib. There for three years, in virtual confinement, they remained. The wailing of the little ones could be heard from without. The hearts of many were softened at the privations which the ban occasioned; but relief was long of coming.

Jewish history embodied in the Coran.

It must have been about this time that Mahomet obtained a closer acquaintance with Jewish history and tradition, either from those whom he met at the season of pilgrimage, or from some Hebrew

[1] *Lahab* signifying "flame."

captive detained at Mecca. The chapters of the Coran belonging to this period begin to teem with lengthy narrations of the Creation, Fall, Flood, &c., as also of the patriarchs, kings, and prophets, all betraying an intimate acquaintance with Jewish lore. The Coreish cast it in his teeth, saying:—"These are fables of the ancients, which he hath had written down; they are dictated unto him morning and evening." To which Mahomet made rejoinder, "The tongue of him whom they mean is a foreign tongue, whereas this revelation is in purest Arabic;"—hardly, it will be thought, a conclusive answer.

Sura xxv. 5.

Christianity as yet little noticed.

We meet with little or no mention of Christianity in the Suras yet put forth.

CHAPTER VII.

THE BAN REMOVED—DEATH OF KHADIJA AND ABU TALIB—MARRIAGE WITH SAUDA AND BETROTHAL TO AYESHA. ÆTAT. 51, 52.

Roll of ban eaten up of ants.

THE three years of detention in the Quarter of Abu Tâlib passed wearily. The sympathies of many were stirred, and they grieved at the rupture. At last it came to the ears of Mahomet that the roll in which the ban was written had been defaced by ants. Abu Tâlib, on hearing this, went forth from his retirement and proceeded to the Káaba. A knot of the leading men were as usual gathered there. The aged chief told them of the ominous fact he had discovered, and upbraided them with their inhumanity and their breach of social obligations. Having thus delivered himself, he withdrew behind the curtain that shrouded the Káaba, prayed there for deliverance, and straightway retired from whence he came.

Abu Tâlib upbraids the Coreish.

Ban removed: ætat. 51.

The murmurs of the sympathizers now found utterance. The company had hardly recovered from the sudden apparition and reproach of Abu Tâlib, when five of them arose, and declaring themselves against the league, put on their armour and repaired to the gateway leading into the defile of Abu Tâlib. They commanded all that had taken refuge there to go forth to their homes, under their guarantee, in security and peace. So they went forth in the tenth year of the ministry of Mahomet.

Death of Khadîja, A.D. 619: ætat. 51.

But the respite was not long enjoyed by the prophet in tranquillity and rest. His home was destined soon to be broken up.. His daughters had married and gone away to their husbands' houses, excepting Fâtima, the youngest, between whom and Aly, her father's cousin, an attachment was already springing up. And now, within a few months of the cancelment of the ban, Khadîja sickened and died. Her virtues are still held in veneration, and her tomb, in the valley just above the city, is visited to the present day by Moslem pilgrims. Not long after, Abu Tâlib too passed away. As he felt life to be ebbing, he summoned his brethren, and commended his nephew to their guardianship. He was buried near to Khadîja, and Mahomet wept as he followed the bier. For forty years his uncle had been his faithful friend, the stay of his early life, and in the later days of trial a strong tower of defence. Another Khadîja might perchance be found, but not a second Abu Tâlib.

And of Abu Tâlib, A.D. 620.

Mahomet visits Tâyif.

Even Abu Lahab was touched by the appeal of the dying patriarch. But his sympathy was short-lived; for he soon again deserted his nephew. Though the ban no longer divided the society of Mecca, the prospects of the faith were not encouraging. There had for long been no new adhesions of consequence to the cause. A few more years of similar discouragement, and all chance of success would be gone. Mahomet looked around if haply help might come from any quarter. And first he turned his eyes to Tâyif,—a town sixty or seventy miles eastwards, on the borders of the table-land,—a spot smiling with fountains, vineyards, and gardens. Though related to the Coreish, the citizens were jealous of them. They had a tutelary Lât or idol of their own, with its rival worship. A cause rejected by Mecca, and appealing to their tribal pride, might obtain from them a favourable hearing. And so Mahomet, attended by Zeid alone, set out on the adventurous journey, Jonah-like, summoning Târif to repentance. But the rulers, insensible to the appeal, bade him to seek support elsewhere, and the common people heaped insult on his head. After ten days of vain endeavour, his departure was hastened by the rabble. They hooted him and Zeid through the streets, and pelted them with stones. Blood flowed from the limbs of Mahomet, and his companion was wounded in the head. Pursued thus for several miles, they found refuge in a vineyard. It belonged to two rich men of the Coreish, who had gardens (as the citizens of Mecca still have) in the vale of Târif. These, having compassion on the fugitives, sent them a tray of grapes. Mahomet was refreshed by the cooling fruit, but still more by the kind words of a Christian slave who brought them to him. Comforted thus, he betook himself to prayer. The petitions, ascribed to him on the occasion, may be taken as indicating the depth of his distress and the faith that served to sustain him. And thus, we are told, he prayed:—

Is expelled by the rabble.

His prayer by the way.

O Lord, I make my complaint unto Thee of my helplessness and insignificance. But Thou art the Lord of the poor and feeble, and Thou art my Lord. To whom wilt Thou abandon me? Into the hands of Strangers that beset me round about, or of the Enemy whom Thou hast given at home the mastery over me? If Thy wrath be not upon me, I have no concern, but rather Thy favour compasseth me the wider about. I seek for refuge in the light of Thy countenance. It is Thine to show anger until that Thou art pleased. It is Thine to chase away the darkness. There is none other power nor is there any resource but in Thee!

And reassured thus, he again set out on the road leading back to Mecca.

Half-way lay the vale of Nakhla, with an idol fane and shady grove. Dreading the reception which, after his bootless mission to the rival city, he might meet with at home, he halted there. The occasion is memorable, for while waiting at Nakhla there appeared to the excited mind of Mahomet, whether in a dream or in a trance, a company of the Genii, the *Jinn* of Eastern romance. They pressed, he tells us, round about him to hear the preaching of Islam. The grotesque scene is thus pictured in the Coran:—

Audience of the Genii at Nakhla.

And do thou call to mind when WE caused a Company of the Genii to turn aside unto thee, listening to the Coran. When they were present at the revelation thereof, they said one to another, *Give ear.* And when it was ended they returned to their people preaching. They said, "O our people! we have been listening to a Book sent down since the days of Moses, which attesteth the truth of the Scriptures preceding it. O our people, obey the preacher of God, that the Lord may forgive you your sins and save you from a fearful doom."

Sura xlvi.

And again:—

Say:—It hath been revealed unto me that a company of Genii listened; and they said, "Verily we have heard a marvellous discourse.

Sura lxxii.

"It guideth to the right direction. Wherefore we believed therein. Henceforth we will associate none other with the Lord. Verily He hath taken no spouse, neither hath He any offspring;"—

And so on at considerable length, the Genii in this curious passage speaking the language of true Moslems.

From Nakhla Mahomet sent messages once and again to Mecca, praying that the protection of some leading citizen might be given him for safe conduct home, but without success. At last he bethought him of one who had generously helped to break the ban. This chief forthwith arose, and buckling on his armour, took his stand with a band of retainers by the Káaba. Assured of his guarantee, the two wanderers returned; and Mahomet having kissed the Black Stone, went back, still guarded by the chief, to his home.

Mahomet's return to Mecca.

The outlook was dark. If help should not come from elsewhere, there was little hope of success at Mecca. Meanwhile, amid trial and discouragement, Mahomet sought solace in fresh nuptials. Sauda, the lady on whom he now set his affections, was of mature age, widow of one of the Abyssinian refugees. The marriage took place just two or three months after Khadîja's death. About the same time Mahomet betrothed to himself Ayesha, the daughter of his friend Abu Bekr. She was then only six or seven years of age. But there must have been something more than ordinarily precocious about the child which led to her marriage within three or four years from this time.

Marries Sauda and is betrothed to Ayesha: ætat. 51.

Mahomet still continued to dwell in the Quarter of Abu Tâlib, but no longer in the affluence of his early married life. What had become of the wealth of Khadîja we are not told. During the late troubles, and the distress of the ban, it had probably melted away. And there are not wanting indications at this period of even straitened means.

Straitened circumstances.

The season of pilgrimage again came round, and Mahomet, as his wont was, plied the crowds of devotees wherever he saw a likely audience. The rites were nearly over, and the multitudes about to disperse, when in the valley of Mina the preacher met a group of six or seven men whom he recognized as citizens of Medina. "What tribe are ye of?" said he, accosting them kindly. "Of the Beni Khazraj," they replied. "Ah! confederates of the Jews. Why not sit ye down a little with me, and I will speak with you?" They sat down, he expounded to them his doctrine, and they listened gladly. Then he set forth his difficulties at home, and asked whether they would receive him at Medina. "Thy teaching we commend," they said; "but as for receiving thee, our tribes have been, as thou dost know, at deadly feud among themselves, and that might hinder us. Let us return to our people. Haply the Lord may restore peace amongst us. And we will come back to thee at this set time next year."

At pilgrimage Mahomet meets enquirers from Medina: A.D. 602, ætat. 52.

A gleam of hope shot across the path of Mahomet. Might it be that the long-looked-for succour was to come from thence?

Gleam of hope.

CHAPTER VIII.

PLANTING OF ISLAM AT MEDINA.

Medina founded by Jews and Arabs.

MEDINA, the ancient *Yathrib*, on the highway between Mecca and Syria, was founded by Jewish tribes, which at an early period of our era found refuge there from the troubles in Palestine. After a time, but still several centuries before our present history, two Arab tribes, the Beni Aus and Khazraj, journeying in the great emigration then taking place northward from Yemen, also settled here. The Jews, worsted by these Arabs, retired without the city and established themselves in three strongholds, which thus were occupied severally by the Jewish clans named Coreitza, Nadhîr, and Caynocâa. The Arabs, in process of time, fell to deadly feud among themselves, and, while Mahomet preached at Mecca, had been waging sanguinary conflict with each other. In their warfare they sought assistance from the Jews, who joined the intestine struggle, some on the side of the Beni Aus, some on the side of the Beni Khazraj.

Medina a likely soil for the new religion.

Such was Medina at the present moment, ready to welcome an adventurer from without. A city addicted to the superstition of the Káaba, yet familiar with the Jewish faith, was in the best state of preparation to throw in its lot with one who, while acknowledging Judaism, aimed also at the reformation of the Meccan worship. In their days of depression the Jews had been wont to tell their Arab fellow-citizens that they looked for a prophet who was predicted in their books to arise and rid them of their adversaries. The vague expectation of a coming dispensation was thus bruited abroad, and Mahomet was not slow to avail himself of it. The Coreish were well known at Medina, as they passed to and fro with their Syrian caravans, and the citizens themselves frequented Mecca at the seasons of annual pilgrimage. Moreover, through the marriage of Hâshim, his father's grandfather, with a lady of Medina, Mahomet himself had the blood of the Beni Khazraj in his veins. Jealousies at home might well extinguish jealousy of the stranger. The city, weary with strife and faction, would be ready to admit Mahomet as a refugee, if not to welcome him as a prophet,—it might even be as her future chief.

A year of anxious waiting for Mahomet: A.D. 620.

Despite hopes like these, the year following the interview above described was for Mahomet one of anxious waiting. Would the little knot of enquirers hold steadily by the cause? Would they succeed in winning adherents from amongst their fellow-citizens? Would Medina receive him, or might he be forced to flee elsewhere, and, like the Abyssinian exiles, seek refuge at some Christian court? Such were the doubts which must have exercised his soul. But when, at the ensuing pilgrimage, he sought the appointed spot in the vale of Mina, his fears vanished forthwith. Twelve citizens of note, representing both the Aus and Khazraj tribes, were ready there to pledge their faith to him.

The first pledge of Acaba: A.D. 621.

This they did, swearing that they would not worship any but the One true God; that they would not steal, neither commit adultery, nor kill their children; that they would slander no one; neither would they disobey the prophet in anything that was right. On his part, Mahomet gave the promise from his Lord, of a place in paradise for all that should remain faithful. This is known as "the first pledge of *Acaba*,"—so called from the "defile" where for secrecy they held their conference in the dead of night. A mosque still marks the spot, hard by the pilgrim road.

Spread of Islam at Medina: A.D. 621.

The twelve were now committed to the cause of Mahomet. They returned to Medina the missionaries of Islam, binding themselves to report progress again at the following pilgrimage. So good was the ground, and the propagation so zealous, that the faith spread from house to house and from tribe to tribe. The Jews looked on in amazement. The people whom they had for ages sought in vain to convert from the errors of polytheism, were now casting their idols to the moles and to the bats, and professing belief in the One only God. The secret lay in the aptness of the instrument. It was native and congenial. Judaism, foreign in its birth, touched no Arab sympathies. Islam, grafted on the faith and superstition, the customs and nationality of the Arabs, gained ready access to their hearts.

A teacher sent to Medina.

The leaders in the movement soon found themselves unable to keep pace with its rapid spread. They wrote to Mahomet for a teacher, able to recite the Coran, and instruct enquirers in the faith. A young disciple was sent, who found the converts already in the habit of assembling themselves together for prayer and the reading of the word. For the first time the combined devotions of the rival clans (for even in their worship they had as yet been impatient of a common leader) were now conducted by the youthful missionary. So speedily did Islam grow and multiply at Medina; and thus widely and unexpectedly were the people prepared for a greater demonstration at the next time of pilgrimage.

CHAPTER IX.

ANOTHER YEAR AT MECCA—A PROPHECY AND A VISION.
A.D. 621.

Continued antagonism at Mecca.

MEANWHILE things went on at Mecca pretty much as before. Mahomet continued to give forth his message; indeed, he began to deliver it in much greater volume than before. Long-spun stories, often following closely the Books of Moses, the Talmud, and Arab legend, are told as lessons to edify the believer or to warn the ungodly Meccans. Solemn denunciations of the Divine wrath in the world to come, are followed by threats of an even nearer punishment which might haply overwhelm the stiff-necked and wicked citizens in the present life. Though wanting, as a rule, in its ancient fire, the oracle is still couched in language often of marvellous force and beauty; and, in fact, Mahomet advances his Revelation as a miracle of rhetoric, challenging his adversaries to produce "ten chapters," or even a single one, the like thereof. Its verses are each a "sign" of Divine inspiration to the unbeliever.[1] In their turn, the Meccans defy the threatened vengeance, and deride the message as "a lesson taught by some foreign prompter, or the mere effusion of a frenzied poet."

[1] The word "verse" means in the Arabic also a "sign." For such challenges see Suras x. 38; xi. 14, &c.

The prospect of finding a refuge in Medina, and thus moving closer to the Syrian border, quickened the interest of Mahomet in the fortunes of the Byzantine empire. For several years the arms of Persia had been turned successfully against the Roman border. Syria was ravaged, Jerusalem sacked, Egypt and Asia Minor overrun. The enemy advanced upon the Bosphorus, and there for ten years a Persian camp was pitched almost within sight of Constantinople. About the time of the first Pledge of Acaba, while the fortunes of Byzantium were at their lowest ebb, Mahomet uttered a sagacious augury of the eventual success of the Kaisar, on whose side were at this time enlisted his hopes and sympathies. The passage opens with these words:—

Prophecy that Heraclius would beat the Persians.

> The Greeks have been smitten
> In the neighbouring coasts;
> But after their defeat they shall again be victorious
> In a few years. To God belongeth the matter from before and after. . .
> He aideth whom He chooseth, the GLORIOUS, the MERCIFUL!
> It is the promise of the Lord, who changeth not His promise.

Sura xxx.

And the prophecy was justified by the event; for just about this time Heraclius, roused from his ignoble slumber, began to roll back the invasion, and in the end totally discomfited the Persians.

It must have been now also that Mahomet gained, either from Christian slaves at Mecca, or at the neighbouring fairs, or perchance from fragments of the Gospels, such as those copied out by Waraca, some acquaintance with the outlines of our Saviour's life. A few of the episodes, those especially connected with the birth of John the Baptist and

Relations of Mahomet with Christianity.

of Jesus Himself, are given in the Coran with much detail, and sometimes in the very words of the Evangelist. But all this and also certain of the miracles are overlaid with many childish legends. Moreover, the sonship and the death of Jesus, as well as the doctrine of the Trinity, are strenuously denied.[1] In other respects the religion is favourably spoken of, and the Gospel, like the Law, is appealed to as the light and guide of mankind. But, while, on the one hand, the attitude of Mahomet towards Christians never became embittered, as afterwards was the case towards his Jewish neighbours at Medina; so likewise, on the other hand, his acknowledgment of the Gospel, probably even his acquaintance with its teaching, never advanced beyond the point at which we find the same embodied in his utterances at the present time. Indeed, if we except an occasional campaign against some distant Christian tribe, or the reception of a Christian embassy, he did not at any period of his life come into close contact with the professors of the Gospel, and it is doubtful whether he had even any intelligible perception of the leading tenets of the faith of Jesus. Neither baptism nor the Lord's Supper are at all alluded to in the Coran, unless, indeed, the tale of the Table sent down from heaven at the prayer of Jesus should refer to the latter.[2]

The midnight journey to Jerusalem and ascent to heaven.

The famous romance of the heavenly journey belongs to this expectant period. Jerusalem was throughout his ministry regarded by Mahomet with the utmost veneration. Indeed, until his removal to Medina and the breach that followed

[1] The Moslems hold that it was a phantom, and not the real person of Jesus, that was crucified.

[2] Sura v. 123.

with the Jews, the temple of Solomon was his *Kibla*, that is to say, the place towards which, at each stated time of genuflexion, he turned to pray. Now even in his dreams the thoughts of Mahomet were veering northwards. The musings of the day reappeared in the slumbers of the night. He dreamed that in the company of Gabriel he was borne swiftly on a winged steed from Mecca to Jerusalem, where a conclave of the ancient prophets met to welcome him. Thence mounting upward, he ascended from heaven to heaven one after another, till at last, reaching the seventh, he found himself in the awful presence of his Maker, and was dismissed with the behest that his people should prostrate themselves in prayer five times in the day. When he awoke in the morning, the vision was imprinted on his memory with all the freshness of reality. He told his family and every one around, that during the night he had been praying in the temple at Jerusalem. Unbelievers derided, and disciples were staggered; some even went back. But Abu Bekr declared his implicit faith in the journey as a simple matter of fact; and in the end the cause sustained no harm. Tradition decks out the tale in gorgeous drapery; and upon the rock on which the Mosque of Omar stands in Jerusalem, there is still shown the print of Mahomet's foot as he vaulted therefrom upon his winged steed. Such are the vagaries of tradition. But the only mention of the journey in the Coran is in the following verse:—

> Praise be to Him who by night carried His servant from the sacred temple at Mecca to the Further temple the environs whereof WE have blessed, that WE might show him some of OUR signs. Verily he it is that heareth and that seeth. Sura xvii.

CHAPTER X.

SECOND PLEDGE OF ACABA—FLIGHT TO MEDINA.

A.D. 622. ÆTAT. 52, 53.

Second deputation from Medina: March 622.

THUS passed another year away. Mahomet, like one of the prophets of Israel, held his people at bay. The spectacle was grand, but still no advance was made in the conversion of Mecca to his creed. Meanwhile tidings continually arrived of the marvellous growth of Islam at Medina. The season of pilgrimage again drew near, and preparations were made for a more numerous embassage than before, and for a yet more decisive demonstration of allegiance to the person and the cause of Mahomet. But the occasion was critical. The Coreish might construe the countenance of strangers into hostile intrusion, and the sword might be unsheathed too soon. It was needful to proceed with the utmost caution. The meeting was again to be by night, and also at the close of the pilgrim rites, when, the sacrifices being ended, the multitudes would at once disperse. The spot was the same secluded glen, at the entrance of the vale of Mina, where the first pledge was taken. Thither the disciples from Medina were silently to wend their way after others had gone to rest, "neither awakening the sleeper, nor yet tarrying for the loiterer."

Mahomet meets the disciples from Medina.

At midnight Mahomet attended only by his uncle Abbâs—still an unbeliever, but (as Abu Tâlib was) attached to the person of his nephew,—repaired to the rendezvous, the first of the party. For greater safety, none of the disciples from Mecca was present; the meeting was kept profoundly secret even from them. The prophet had not long to wait. For now, in the light of the full moon, might be seen stealing thither along the stony glen, under cover of its barren rocks, the men of Medina, singly and in twos and threes. They were in all seventy-three men and two women. When all were seated on the ground, Abbâs in a low voice addressed them. His own clan, he said, even such as like himself held by their ancestral faith, were ready as heretofore to defend his nephew. "But he hath chosen rather," continued Abbâs, "to seek the refuge which ye offer him. Wherefore, consider the matter well, and count the cost. If it be your will, and ye have the means withal, be it so; otherwise, at once abandon the design." He paused, and Berâ, an aged chief, stepped forth. "Our resolve," he said, "is fixed and irreversible. Life and property are at the prophet's service. It is the time for him to speak."

The Second pledge of Acaba.

Mahomet began by setting forth his faith in passages taken from the Coran. Then he called upon all to embrace the cause of the Lord, and share in the blessings of Islam. He would be content, he said, if they should pledge their faith to defend him as they would their own wives and children. A tumultuous noise arose. It was the eager voices of the seventy professing readiness to pledge themselves to Mahomet at the risk of life and property. "Hush!" cried Abbâs; "there may be spies abroad. Here" (holding his nephew's hand), "let your men of years come forth and speak. Then pledge your troth and haste away." Berâ again advanced and said, "Stretch forth thy hand, O Mahomet!" And then Berâ struck his hand upon the extended palm of Mahomet, as the manner was in taking the oath of fealty. After him the Seventy came forward, one by one, and did the same. When all had passed thus, Mahomet chose out Twelve chief men from amongst them, saying, "Ye shall be the leaders and the sureties of the rest, even as the apostles of Jesus were sureties for His people." Just then a cry was heard—a straggler perchance seeking for his company; but to the excited assembly it seemed a spy of the Coreish, if not the devil's emissary, seeking to betray them. In alarm, they all broke up and hurried back to their several companies. And so ended the Second pledge of Acaba.

The Coreish challenge the Medina chiefs.

Rumours of the gathering were not long in reaching the ears of the Coreish, who in the morning repaired to the encampment of the Medina citizens, and demanded the explanation of what seemed to be a conspiracy, amounting indeed to a hostile movement, against them. But the bulk of the men of Medina were in ignorance of what had passed, and such even as knew protested that their accusers had been misinformed. The assembly of pilgrims broke up without any further question. But during the day the facts transpired, and the roads were scoured, in the hope of securing some of the unfriendly visitors. Two were seized and dragged back to Mecca, but at the intercession of friends were set at liberty.

It could no longer be concealed that Mahomet and his followers contemplated an early flight. That their enemies should escape to an asylum beyond their reach, from whence to plot revenge, kindled the wrath of the Coreish. They renewed their persecution, and sought to force the confessors to recant, or else by confinement to prevent escape. This hastened the crisis. It was not long after the memorable night of the Second Acaba that Mahomet gave his followers leave to quit their native city. "Depart to Medina," he said, "for the Lord verily hath given you brethren there, and a home wherein ye may take refuge." And so they began to leave stealthily, in small companies, some on camels and some on foot. The journey of two hundred and fifty miles is done by caravans in ten or twelve days. By the end of two months, nearly all the followers of Mahomet, excepting such as were detained against their will, had migrated to their new abode. With their families they numbered about one hundred and fifty souls. They were received with a hearty welcome by their brethren at Medina, who vied with one another for the honour of lodging them in their homes and supplying their domestic needs. The people of Mecca looked on amazed, as family after family silently disappeared, and house after house was left empty. At last Mahomet and Abu Bekr, with their households, were all that remained. Abu Bekr, who was to be the companion of the prophet in his flight, was impatient to leave, but Mahomet told him that his time was not yet come. Two swift camels were kept by Abu Bekr in readiness tethered in his yard, and intrusted to a guide familiar with the devious paths on the Medina road.

Followers of Mahomet emigrate to Medina: April, May, A.D. 622.

Mahomet, Abu Bekr, and Aly remain behind.

The Coreish were perplexed as to what might be the prophet's meaning. Remaining almost solitary behind, did he challenge or defy attack? They assembled in conclave to deliberate what was the wisest course; whether to seize and cast him into prison, or to expel him from their coasts? The more hostile took counsel, it is said, even to put him to death. But nothing was determined. They agreed at last to send a deputation to his house,—with what precise object, amidst the mazes of tradition, it is hard to say. We are told that the devil, in guise of an aged stranger, shrouded in a mantle, appeared in the council to support Abu Jahl,[1] the arch-enemy of Mahomet, in compassing his death. But in the passage where the prophet himself mentions the crisis, the design of his enemies is stated only in these indecisive terms:—

Council of the Coreish.

> The unbelievers plotted that they might *detain thee, or slay thee, or expel thee.* But the Lord plotted likewise, and He is the best of plotters.

Sura viii. 29.

Whatever their object, the visitors found Mahomet gone. He had stolen away; and, to disarm suspicion, had thrown his own red mantle over Aly, and left him lying thus upon his bed. From thence he had gone straightway to the house of Abu Bekr, who shed tears of joy that the hour had come, and he was now to be the companion of his Master's flight. In the shade of evening they crept through a back window, and emerged from the city unobserved. Directing their steps over the hills to the south, they clambered in the dark for two or three hours the bare and rugged ascent,

Mahomet and Abu Bekr escape to Mount Thaur.

[1] This was not his proper name, but a sobriquet which the Moslems gave him,—"Father of Ignorance or folly," in token of his dogged opposition to their prophet.

and reaching at last the lofty peak of Mount Thaur, took refuge in a cavern near the summit, hidden by the rocks. Here they rested secure; for the attention of their enemies, they knew, would be directed to the pathways leading north.

The Coreish baulked.

The city was in a ferment when the news of Mahomet's disappearance spread abroad. When the chiefs reached his house, and asked Aly where his cousin was, he made answer, "Am I his keeper? Ye bade him go, and he hath gone." Scouts were sent in all directions, but the search was fruitless. One by one they returned with no tidings of the fugitives. They had gained a fair start, no doubt, and had outstripped pursuit. And Mecca breathed more freely, now her troubler was gone.

Mahomet and Abu Bekr in the cave.

Legends of miracles cluster about the cave. The spider wove her web across its mouth. Branches sprouted over the opening; wild pigeons settled on them to divert attention, and so forth. We may question whether there was any real danger, but Mahomet and Abu Bekr no doubt felt it to be a time of jeopardy. When the morning light broke through a crevice overhead, Abu Bekr whispered, "What if they were to look through the chink and see us at their feet?" "Think not thus," answered Mahomet. "We are two, but God is in our midst a Third."

Several years after, the occasion was thus alluded to in the Coran:—

Reference to cave in Coran.

If ye will not assist the Prophet, verily the Lord assisted him aforetime, when the unbelievers cast him forth in the company of a Second only. When they Two were in the cave alone; when the Prophet said to his Companion, *Be not cast down, verily God is with us.* And the Lord caused peace to descend upon him, and strengthened him with Hosts that ye saw not, &c.

The "Second of the Two" became one of Abu Bekr's most honoured titles, as a contemporary poet of Medina sang:—

The Second of the Two.

And the Second of the Two in the glorious Cave, while around the foes were searching; and the Two had ascended the mountain together.

And they knew that the Prophet loved him above all the world beside; he held no one equal to him.

The excitement over in Mecca, the sooner the fugitives should now quit their retreat the better. Delay might attract suspicion; for every night in the dark, the son and servant of Abu Bekr brought milch goats and food to the mouth of the cave. On the third day, therefore, the guide was bidden to be in readiness on the following evening with the camels near the summit of the hill. At dusk Abu Bekr's daughter, Asma, brought a wallet filled with food for the way. She had forgotten the thong to fasten it, so she tore her girdle in two. With one strip she closed the wallet, and with the other she bound it to the saddle. From this act Asma is known throughout Islam as "She of the Two Shreds."[1] Abu Bekr carried with him a bag containing 5000 dirhems[2]—all that remained to him of his fortune.

Preparations for the journey.

On the evening of the fourth day, quitting their concealment, they mounted the camels,—Mahomet on Al Caswa, the swifter of the two, with the guide in front; Abu Bekr and his servant on the other. Descending the hills, they left Mecca on

Flight of Mahomet: A.D. 622, A.H. I.: ætat. 53.

[1] She was mother to Zobeir, and survived his rebellion. See 'Annals of the Early Caliphate,' p. 446.

[2] Say from two to three hundred pounds sterling.

the right, and hastening westward, struck into the by-ways leading toward the sea-shore. It was the 25th of June, A.D. 622, or the fourth day of the third Arabian month of the first year of the *Hegira*, or Flight.[1]

By daybreak they reached a Bedouin encampment, where an Arab widow sat at her tent-door with viands spread out for the chance traveller. Fatigued and thirsty, for it was now the hottest season of the year, they refreshed themselves with the food and draughts of milk offered by the lady. In the evening, being now, as they deemed, at a safe distance, they fell into the common road. They had not gone far when they met one of the scouts on horseback, returning from his search. But the party was too strong for him, and they passed each other. On the third day a caravan appeared in sight. It was Talha, a young and early convert, cousin of Abu Bekr, on his way back from a trading trip to Syria. After warm greetings, Talha opened his stores, and gave the soiled and weary travellers two changes of white raiment. Yet more welcome was the assurance that he had left the disciples at Medina eagerly looking for their prophet. So the fugitives journeyed onwards with lightened heart and quickened pace.

The journey.

Aly remained three days at Mecca after Mahomet had quitted the cave, and then prepared leisurely to follow. The families of the

Families left behind at Mecca.

[1] Hegira (note that the *i* is short) signifies "flight," or "emigration." The Hegira, as a conventional era, was not established till some years after by Omar, the second Caliph. It counts from *Moharram*, that is, from the first month of the Arabian calendar, or two months before the actual flight from the cave. The Arabian is a purely lunar year, which (being eleven days shorter than the solar year) gains one year in every thirty-three years of our computation.

prophet and of Abu Bekr were still left behind. Rockeya had gone away to Abyssinia with her husband. The rest continued for the present at Mecca, protected, no doubt, by their respective clans. The hostile feeling had calmed down, and we hear of no attempt to injure or insult them.

Thus ends the first period in the life of Mahomet.

MEDINA AT THE PRESENT DAY.

CHAPTER XI.

ARRIVAL AT MEDINA—BUILDING OF THE MOSQUE. JUNE A.D. 622—JAN. 623. A.H. I. ÆTAT. 53.

MEDINA[1] is due north of Mecca, but as the shore northwards trends here considerably west, it is by so much the further from the sea. The direct road from Mecca to Syria, hugging the sea-shore, passes close to Yenbo, the port of Medina. Another route, branching off from Bedr eastward, takes Medina on the way, and by this road the traveller must toil upwards several thousand feet through steep defiles. The mountain tops rise successively before him, till, about a hundred miles from the sea, the margin of the great plain of Nejd is attained, which stretches away, a dry and stony steppe, towards the Persian Gulf. On the border of this plain, and therefore at a considerable elevation above the level of the sea, lies the ancient Yathrib, *Al-Medina*, "*the* city," as by pre-eminence it is called. Its site is a little lower than the crest of the western mountains up which the wayfarer has climbed, and which therefore turn the drainage eastward. The town lies in a shallow basin, towards which the waters from the

Medina.

[1] Pronounced *Medeena.*

hill Ohod and the rising ground to the north converge. Hence the soil is humid; the air, in marked contrast with Mecca, moist; and the weather often, from the altitude, cold and inclement. In striking contrast also to the bare surroundings of the Káaba is the expanse of green fields watered from the abounding wells and springs, and the famous groves of the date tree. At the north-east corner a rugged spur touches the town, which, substantially built, presents along the northern and western sides a strong walled front. On the south, a sheet of verdant gardens extends for a mile or two to the suburb of Coba. Outside the city, at some little distance, were also at this time the three fortified settlements of the Jewish tribes already mentioned.

Mahomet's arrival at Coba: Monday, June 28, A.D. 622.

For several days the citizens had been in expectation of their illustrious guest. They had heard of his disappearance from Mecca, but no one knew of his withdrawal to the cave. Travelling rapidly, he should have arrived before now. The Medina converts and Meccan refugees issued forth daily at early dawn to the heights above the city, straining their eyes to get first sight of the travellers on the Mecca road, and so remained till driven home by the heat of the summer sun. At last one day at noon, when the company of watchers had retired, a Jew perceived the strangers wending their way to Coba, and shouted from his house-top that the long-looked-for travellers had come. They had indeed arrived. Amid the greeting of old friends and the smile of new faces they alighted in the suburb of Coba, and sat down wearied, under the shadow of a tree. The journey had by hasty marches been accomplished in eight days.

Speedily the news spread. The city was moved. The very children in the streets cried out with delight that the prophet had come. From all quarters the disciples hastened to Coba, and made obeisance to Mahomet. He received them courteously. "Show your joy," he said, "by giving around you the salutation of peace: send portions to the poor; bind close the ties of kinsmanship, and pray while others slumber. So shall ye enter Paradise." With Abu Bekr he remained four days under the hospitable roof of friends at Coba, during which time Aly arrived. Here too he laid the foundation of the first house of prayer for his people at Medina, which is honoured in the Coran by the title of "the Mosque of Godly Fear."

He stays four days at Coba.

It was on a Monday he arrived at Coba. Rested now by his stay there, on the following Friday morning Mahomet mounted Al Caswa, with Abu Bekr seated behind him, and, followed by a great multitude, took the way to the city. On the road he halted and performed the first public service with about a hundred worshippers. After prayer there was a sermon or address, in which he spoke in eulogy of the Faith, and bade his people to observe its precepts. Friday was thenceforward set apart for the more special celebration of public worship. The spot, still shown to the pilgrim, is marked by a temple, called in memory of the event, *Masjid al Juma*, "the Friday Mosque."

Leaves Coba for Medina.

First Friday sermon.

The service ended, Mahomet resumed his progress. He had sent word to his kinsfolk of the Beni Khazraj, descendants of the house of Salma (mother of Abd al Muttalib), to escort him into the city. But there was no need of any message. The citizens

Triumphal entry into the city.

streamed forth in crowds. On either side were the chiefs of Medina clad in armour and holiday attire. The procession threaded its way through the groves and gardens of the southern suburb, and as it entered the streets, one after another, with loud voice, invited the strangers to alight and abide with them. So urgent was the call, that they seized the camel's halter. "Let Al Caswa free!" cried Mahomet; "the decision rests with her; make way!" Thus with firm but kindly words he disarmed the jealousies of the rival factions, and, professing to commit his destination into higher hands, continued his way. Onwards Al Caswa moved with slackened rein, and turning to the eastern quarter, entered an open court, stopped of her own accord, and knelt down. Abu Ayûb, one of the covenanters of Al Acaba, whose house was hard by, invited him to enter. Dishes of choice viands presently crowded in from every side, and the same hospitality was maintained so long as Mahomet resided there. For seven months the prophet remained the guest of Abu Ayûb, while his own house was building.[1]

Mahomet alights at the house of Abu Ayûb.

The first concern of the prophet was to secure the ground on which Al Caswa halted. An overgrown, neglected spot, with a few date trees and thorny shrubs, it had been partly used for burial of the dead, and partly for tethering camels. The price was paid by Abu Bekr, and arrangements made forthwith to erect thereon a house of prayer; and also to build by the side of its court two habitations, one for Sauda his wife, the other for Ayesha his bride elect.

Arrangements to build Mosque and houses.

[1] The same Abu Ayûb was killed fifty years after at Constantinople, where his grave is honoured to the present day.

The ground was cleared, an oozing spring was blocked and drained, the graves were dug up and the bones removed; and then a store of sun-dried bricks and other materials was got in readiness for the work.

Mahomet is joined by his family from Mecca.

Mahomet's next care was to send for his family from Mecca. Zeid, deputed for the purpose, met with no opposition from the Coreish, and returned with the households both of the prophet and of Abu Bekr. Mahomet's eldest daughter chose to remain at Mecca with her husband. Rockeya had already reached Medina with Othmân direct from Abyssinia. There remained two other daughters;—Omm Kolthum, who, separated from her husband, a son of Abu Lahab, had for some time been living in her father's house, and her younger sister Fatima, who was still unmarried. These accompanied Sauda and Ayesha to Medina, and were accommodated in houses adjoining that of Abu Ayûb.

Building of Great Mosque.

The converts all laboured in building the Mosque. Their zeal was quickened by Mahomet, who himself shared in the work. He joined too in the song which his followers chanted with loud and cheerful voice as they bore along their burdens:—

> O Lord, there is no joy but the joy of Futurity;
> O Lord, have mercy on the Citizens and the Refugees.

The site is the same as that now occupied by the Grand Mosque and its square, but the dimensions and style were of course far less pretentious. The court was four-square, each side one hundred cubits; the walls partly stone and partly brick; the roof was borne on the stems of palm trees, and covered over with branches of the same. The *Kibla*, or quarter to which they turned in prayer, was still Jerusalem. Thus, at the time of worship Mahomet stood looking to the north, near that end of the Mosque, with his back to the congregation, who all fell in by rows behind him, facing in the same direction. When the prayers were ended he turned himself round to the people, and if there was occasion for an address or sermon, made it then. On one side of the court there arose a modest row of houses with apartments for each of his wives and daughters. To be near at hand, the chief Companions also built houses for themselves close by the Mosque. Some of these houses, as that of Abu Bekr, formed one side of the court, with doors opening directly upon it.

The Mosque used for worship and for public business.

The present Grand Mosque, with its courts, occupies an area three or four times as great as that of the primitive temple. Asked why he did not build a more substantial roof to the House of prayer, Mahomet made answer, "The thatching is as the thatching of Moses, rafters and branches; verily man's estate is more fleeting even than this." Rude in material and insignificant in size, the Mosque of Mahomet is glorious in the annals of Islam. Here the prophet and his Companions spent the greater part of their time; here the daily service, with its oft-recurring prayers, was first publicly established; and here the great congregation assembled every Friday, and listened with reverence and awe to messages which they believed to come direct from heaven. Here Mahomet planned his victories, received embassies from vanquished and contrite tribes, and issued edicts that struck terror into the hearts of rebellious peoples to the very outskirts of the peninsula. Hard by, in the apartment of Ayesha, he yielded up the ghost, and there, side by side with Abu Bekr and Omar, he lies entombed.

The building, which, with its simple arches and tapering supports, set the type of Saracen architecture, was finished seven months after the arrival of Mahomet in Medina. The adjoining houses for his wives were now also ready, and by the winter, Sauda was established in her new abode. Shortly after, he celebrated his marriage with Ayesha at her father's house in the suburb of Al Sunh, and then brought her to the bridal home alongside that of her "sister" Sauda. Thenceforward the affections of Mahomet were to be shared by a plurality of wives, and his company passed on alternate days in their several houses, for he never had a separate apartment of his own. On the present occasion he humoured the juvenile tastes of his bride, at the time a child not more than ten or eleven years of age. Her playthings were brought to the new abode, and Mahomet joined in her infantile games. But her charms as well of mind as of body must have developed rapidly. Slim and graceful in figure, ready wit and arch vivacity set off personal attractions of no ordinary charm. She enthralled Mahomet. And, though exposed while still a girl to the rivalry in his harem of many beautiful women, she maintained her supremacy in the prophet's affections to the end.

Houses of Mahomet's wives.

Marriage with Ayesha.

CHAPTER XII.

PARTIES AT MEDINA.

A.H. II. A.D. 623.

Four parties at Medina.

As the enthusiasm stirred by the arrival of Mahomet gradually subsided, various sentiments began to be entertained regarding him. The inhabitants were divided sharply into four parties —*Refugees; Citizens,*—that portion, namely, which was converted, or was friendly to the prophet; *Disaffected* citizens; and *Jews.*

I. Refugees.

Those who had forsaken house and home for the sake of the faith were thence named, and ever after known, as *Muhâjerîn*, or REFUGEES,—a title soon to become illustrious in the history of Islam. A devoted band, who had stood by Mahomet in the days of his humiliation at Mecca, these recognized him not only as their prophet, but now took him also for their chief and leader.

II. Citizens, or converts of Medina.

Next come the converts of Medina. They had made less outward sacrifice for Islam; but the pledge of Acaba had bound them equally to the cause, and involved them in serious risks and obligations both at home and abroad. These did not yield to the Refugees either in loyalty to the person of Mahomet, or in enthusiasm for the faith. They soon identified themselves with the Exile in offensive measures against his enemies. In the language of Islam they are called *Ansâr*, or *Helpers;* but as Mahomet soon had other allies, it will be more convenient to style them CITIZENS, or Men of Medina.

III. Hypocrites, or DISAFFECTED.

The body of unconverted inhabitants was at the first neutral, or, if there was ill-humour or dislike, it kept latent and passive. There was no active opposition here, as there had been at Mecca. Nor was the authority of Mahomet over his own adherents, native as well as immigrant, denied. The constitution of society, enabled him to exercise unquestioned power over his own people at Medina, without, for the present, arrogating jurisdiction over others. Still, without show of outward hostility, an undercurrent of discontent and jealousy amongst a large and influential part of the community was not long of setting in. But it failed to check the mysterious influence of the Stranger, or stem the tide of his growing popularity. The circle of Mahomet's followers steadily increased, and before long embraced, nominally at least, nearly the whole city. Idolatry disappeared, and scepticism, overmatched, was fain to hide its head. Real belief, however, was not always of such rapid growth; and, at convenient distance, doubts and regrets found free expression. They had espoused the cause of the Exile (so the murmur ran) only to excite hostility abroad, sow dissension at home, and rivet on their neck the Usurper's yoke. Such covert adversaries are named in the Coran "Hypocrites," or DISAFFECTED. At their head was Abdallah ibn Obey, who at the time of Mahomet's advent was about being chosen, both by the Beni Aus and Khazraj, as their prince. This man specially, and the whole class at large, were highly obnoxious to Mahomet. Dreading their covert machinations, he established a close and searching espionage over both their words and actions, and continually in the Coran fulminated denunciations against them.

On quite a different footing were the three Jewish

IV. Jews.

tribes established without the city. From the first Mahomet had acknowledged the validity of their Scriptures. The worship of Islam was in close accord with Jewish ritual. The *Kibla,* or Holy of holies, to which all turned at prayer, was still Jerusalem. No concession was too great that might secure the countenance and allegiance of the Jews. Accordingly, not long after his arrival, Mahomet entered into a treaty with them, which, both offensive and defensive, guaranteed their safety and independence. For a little while cordiality prevailed. But it soon became evident that Judaism and Islam could not run together. Mahomet rested his claim upon the Jewish books, yet he did not profess to be the prophet for whom they looked. Jesus, he held, was the true Messiah, of whose rejection their forefathers had been guilty. He was himself another and a greater prophet, foretold equally in their Scriptures. The Jews, he said, knew it well; but out of enmity they concealed or garbled the prophecies concerning his advent, while, in point of fact, they recognized him to be the coming prophet, "even as they recognized their own sons." On their part, the Jews as a body remained true to their faith. Their books, they affirmed, contained no warrant for these assumptions of the Ishmaelite. Their Messiah was to be, not of Arabian, but of Israelitish blood, and of the seed of David. And so the expectation that they would accept Mahomet as their prophet, and espouse his cause, came to be miserably disappointed.

But amongst the Jews there were renegades. These did not scruple to attest the claims of Mahomet, and to bear witness that in every point he met the description given of the coming prophet in their sacred books. Their brethren, they would say, jealous at the gift of prophecy passing from them to another people, had hid the proofs of the prophet's mission, or by "dislocating" them from the context, had misinterpreted the clear prediction. Judicial blindness—such was now the preaching of Mahomet—had fallen upon them. Their conscience was seared, and their "hearts enveloped in a thick and callous covering." They were but following the example of their forefathers, who had ever murmured against the Lord, put their prophets to death, and rejected the Christ.

Jewish renegades.

Thus the Jews were a trouble and perplexity to Mahomet. The very people to whose testimony he had so long appealed were now a standing witness against him; and before long hatred culminated into hostility. The portions of the Coran given forth at this period teem with invectives against the Israelites. Tales of their ancestors' folly and disobedience are reiterated at wearisome length. And the conclusion is continually drawn that from first to last the Jews had fulfilled the denunciations of the Bible against them, and were still, as they had always been, a stiff-necked and rebellious race.

Hostile feeling between the Jews and Mahomet.

CHAPTER XIII.

RITES AND ORDINANCES—DOMESTIC LIFE. A.H. I., II. A.D. 622, 623. ÆTAT. 54, 55.

THE new faith touched the outer life of its votaries at every step. Five times a day the believer must turn aside to prayer. On each occasion a similar rite was used. It consisted (as it still consists) in repeating a few petitions or short passages, with a fixed ceremonial of genuflexion and prostration. The prayers in the daytime were ordinarily said in the Mosque by Mahomet and such of his followers as dwelt in the vicinity. They might with equal merit be offered anywhere, at home or by the way, singly or in companies, but ever at the stated times. Mahomet when present always led the prayers himself. Thus a continually recurring round of religious observance was imposed on all. At mid-day on Friday the service took a more public form, when Moslems as a body were expected to attend. The usual service was on this occasion followed by a sermon or address. But though Friday was thus distinguished for special worship, it never was hallowed like the Jewish Sabbath. After the service the people returned to their usual avocations. As yet the teaching of Mahomet was not exclusive of Judaism or Christianity. The professors of either might follow their respective Scriptures and yet be good Moslems. And it is not improbable that at this early period some Jews may have even attended both the Synagogue and the Mosque.

But a year and a half after Mahomet's arrival, a change took place which rendered it impossible for faithful Jews any longer to join in the service of the Moslems. Up to this time, by turning daily to Jerusalem at prayer, Mahomet had paid a continual homage to their faith. But as the breach widened, he resolved that they should no longer be able to cast it in his teeth that he had borrowed his Kibla from them. He would divert the allegiance of his people from Jerusalem and concentrate it upon Mecca. And so tradition tells us that as he longed for the change, it came suddenly upon him, in the very act of worship, by a revelation from heaven. "*We shall cause thee*"—such was the command Mahomet professed to receive—"*to turn towards a Kibla that shall please thee. Turn therefore thy face towards the holy temple of Mecca. Wheresoever ye be, turn your faces towards the same.*" Straightway the prophet, and with him all the worshippers in the Mosque, turned, and facing right round to the south, finished thus the service. Thenceforward Jerusalem was abandoned, and the Káaba became, and has been ever since, the Kibla of Islam. The incident significantly marked a change of policy. The tide hitherto running rapidly towards Judaism and Christianity, now stayed, and turned. Henceforth Islam cast aside the trammels of the Mosiac law, and bound itself up in the worship of Mecca. The Jews, mortified and estranged, charged him with fickleness, and with substituting for the temple of the One true God an idolatrous shrine. Their reproaches he sought to set aside by messages from heaven, which still form part of the Coran. But

Kibla changed to Mecca.

Sura ii. 146.

stronger measures were needed, as in the sequel we shall see, to silence their objections.

The Mueddzin's call to prayer.

Mahomet now bethought him of a suitable call to prayer. Some spoke of the Jewish trumpet, others of the Christian bell, but neither was grateful to the prophet's ear. Then, we are told, a vision appeared to one of his followers, in which an angel desired that a crier should call aloud, "*Allah Akbar!* Great is the Lord! There is no other God but He, and Mahomet is His prophet. Come unto prayer! come unto prayer! come unto salvation! There is no God but the Lord alone." Mahomet forthwith bade his negro servant Bilâl to carry out the Divine behest. Ascending a pinnacle hard by the Mosque, the tall, gaunt African, on the first break of day, with stentorian voice aroused the slumberers around by the appointed call—to which he used to add the words, "Prayer is better than sleep, Prayer is better than sleep." Five times every day the loud cry of the *Adzân* summoned the faithful to their devotions. For twelve centuries the same call has sounded forth from a myriad minarets, and the traveller in the East is still startled from his dreams at early dawn by the shrill cry of the successors of Bilâl awakening the people to their matin prayer.

Fast of Ramadhân.

About the same time Mahomet established an annual Fast. At first, while he yet sought to harmonize his religion with that of the Jews, he enjoined on his followers to observe the great Fast of the Atonement.[1] Now that Judaism was cast aside, he commanded instead that the whole month of Ramadhân[2] should be held as a fast. During the day the obligation is so stringent that, without respect of

[1] Levit. xxiii. 27.

[2] Otherwise pronounced *Ramzân*.

sex or age, from dawn to sunset no indulgence is allowed of any kind,—not a morsel of bread nor even a drop of water may pass the lips. For the sick and for travellers a dispensation is given; but with that exception, a penalty is imposed on every breach. The fast was established in the winter-time, but the season is subject to variation. With the Arabian lunar year, the month shifts round the solar cycle once in every three-and-thirty years. And so, when the fast falls in summer, it presses in tropical countries with extreme severity. Yet, however wholesome the austerity may be, its limitation to the day-time altogether defeats the lesson of self-control, so far, at least, as certain classes of indulgence are concerned.

Eed al Fitr; Festival of breaking the Fast.

As soon as the new moon of the month Shawwâl was seen (and it is still eagerly looked for every year throughout the Moslem world), the restriction ceased, and the next day was celebrated as a festival, the *Eed al Fitr*, or Breaking of the Fast. Thank-offerings for the poor were on that occasion invited by the prophet. A special service of prayer was also appointed in the outskirts of the city. Then afterwards a feast was held in the court of the Great Mosque, when the accumulated offerings were distributed amongst the needy.

Eed al Zoha, or Day of Sacrifice.

Another great festival was now established, called the Day of Sacrifice. At the annual pilgrimage of Mecca, victims have from time immemorial been slain in the vale of Mina at the end of the ceremonies. For the first year at Medina, the occasion passed unnoticed. Instead thereof, Jewish ceremonies being still in favour, sacrifices were offered on the Day of Atonement. But soon after the unfriendly change already noticed, that Day was altogether dropped, and the ceremony shifted to correspond with the day of sacrifice at Mina. Still a remnant of Jewish usage remained, for the prophet continued to offer up two goats, one for the people, the other for himself and his household.[1] At Medina and still throughout the Moslem world, a similar sacrifice takes place on the appointed day, just at the moment when the sacrificial rite is being performed at Mina which closes the Greater Pilgrimage.

The Post for prayer, and the Pulpit.

Mahomet used at the first to pray standing by a post planted in the floor of the Mosque. Seeing him fatigued after a lengthened service, one offered to make for him a pulpit, like those in the churches of Syria, and the thing pleased him. It was soon made up of tamarisk wood, having a seat with three steps leading up to it. The pulpit was placed by the south wall of the Mosque, looking northwards towards the congregation. The post was then, as a sacred relic, buried under the pulpit. The expressions of regret with which the prophet parted from it gave rise to the fond myth of the "Moaning Post;" for, on being set aside, it continued to sigh and groan (so we are told) till Mahomet soothed it into silence by stroking it kindly with his hand.

The "Moaning Post."

Order of Friday service.

The order of Friday service was this. On entering the place of worship, Mahomet ascended the pulpit, and gave the assembly the salutation of peace. He sat down as Bilâl was sounding forth the call to prayer. When this was over, he descended, and took his stand in front of the pulpit, looking towards the Káaba, with his back to the people; then he engaged in prayer, with various forms of genu-

[1] Levit. xvi.; Heb. vii. 27.

flection,—the congregation behind him facing similarly, and following every word and gesture of their leader. The prayers ended, Mahomet usually ascended the pulpit again, and delivered one or more addresses, sitting down between each. He would on such occasions gesticulate in earnest discourse, with outstretched arm and pointed finger. The people, who hung upon his words, would at the close join in a loud Amen. On Fridays and Festivals the prophet was clad in a mantle of striped stuff thrown over his shoulder, with a girdle of fine cloth from Oman bound about his waist. At other times he ministered in his ordinary dress.

Superstitious regard for the pulpit.

The pulpit was held in great reverence. Oaths regarding disputed rights were taken beside it, and Mahomet taught that evidence thus falsely sworn carried its punishment into the future life, "even if the subject were but a toothpick." The sentiment degenerated into superstition, and we are told that an attempt made in the days of the Caliphs to remove the pulpit to Damascus made the earth to quake. Mahomet himself used to speak of the space between the pulpit and his door as "one of the gardens of paradise." The figurative words were soon taken literally, and the fond conceit is perpetuated to the present day by flowery carpeting on the floor, and arabesques to correspond upon the wall.

Simplicity of Mahomet's life.

Mahomet lived a simple life. For each addition to his harem, a room was added to the row of houses which formed one side of the court of the Mosque. They were homely in appearance, built of sun-dried brick, in dimension but twelve or fourteen feet square, with a small veranda, but so low that the roof might be touched with the hand. At the door of

Ayesha's chamber was a closet, where in the evening or at night Mahomet retired for his devotions. The furnishings were in keeping. A leathern mattress stuffed with coir was spread for repose upon the floor. In place of garniture, the walls were hung with skins such as are used in the East to hold milk or water, and when empty are blown out, and so suspended. Abdallah ibn Masûd was the servant who usually attended to the simple wants of the prophet's toilet, took charge of his staff when he went abroad, and when he alighted, of his shoes. Abdallah's mother, once like her son a slave, performed such menial offices as were required by the wives of Mahomet. But meanness and discomfort lay only in contrast with the splendour and luxury of the Caliphs who succeeded him. Bred in the simplicity of Arab life, artificial comforts would have been irksome and uneasy. The prophet was happier with his wives, each in her small and rudely-furnished cabin, than he would have been surrounded with the grandeur and delicacies of a palatial residence.

CHAPTER XIV.

HOSTILITIES WITH MECCA—COMMAND TO FIGHT.

A.H. I., II. A.D. 623.

FOR six or seven months after the Flight, nothing of either a hostile or a friendly character transpired between the two cities. On the one hand, the Coreish planned no vindictive measures against the fugitives, nor did they attempt to molest the followers of the prophet, or the members of his household, left for a time behind. On the other, he himself was fully occupied in settling his household and his people in their new home, and in strengthening his position there. But after several months the time came round when in winter it was customary for the trading caravans to proceed to Syria. These were often richly freighted. In barter for the produce of Arabia laden upon their camels, the inhabitants of Mecca were supplied with the luxuries of the north. The traffic yielded so great a profit, that in some of the larger ventures almost every citizen had a share. When the road was unsafe, the caravan was usually guarded by an armed convoy; and even in times of peace it offered, if unprotected, to the freebooter an easy and a tempting prize. The beaten

Feeling at Mecca.

The caravans passing dangerously near Medina.

path to Syria passed almost within sight of Medina, and thus Mahomet was well placed to watch the movements of the Meccan caravans, and, like an eagle from its eyrie, to swoop down upon his victim.

Three expeditions from Medina. Dec 622 A.D. Feb. 623 A.D. A. H. I.

The earliest attempts of the kind were petty and inconclusive. In the winter of the first year at Medina, three expeditions were despatched in various directions. For each of these Mahomet mounted a white banner upon a staff, and placed it in the hands of the leader. But the numbers were small, in no case exceeding fifty, and they failed either to intercept their prize or to inflict serious injury on the convoys. In the following summer and autumn, Mahomet himself led three somewhat larger but equally unsuccessful parties. These were now joined by some of the citizens of Medina, who thus crossed the Rubicon and identified themselves with the Moslems in the hostile movement. The men of Mecca, on their side, became alive to the danger, increased the guarding convoys, and kept generally on the alert. It was about this time that a richly-laden caravan under command of Abu Sofiân, the chief who had now assumed leadership of the Coreish, passed up on its way to Syria. This is the same caravan which on its return journey some months after gave rise to the famous battle of Bedr.

Three expeditions led by Mahomet: June–Oct. 623. A.H. II.

Affair of Nakhla: Nov. 623. Rajab A. H. II.

During the winter a small foray in another direction ended in more serious results. It was directed against the traffic between Mecca and the south. The expedition consisted of but eight persons. Sealed instructions were given to Abdallah, its leader, to be opened only on reaching a certain spot near to Mecca. "Go forward to Nakhla,"

so the prophet's order ran, "and lie there in wait for a caravan of the Coreish." This was a valley outside the sacred territory, on the Tâyif road, through which the trade with Yemen passed. They had not long to wait, when a caravan came up laden with raisins, wine, and leather. It was guarded by four of the Coreish, who, seeing the strangers, took alarm and halted. It was the last day of Rajab, a month sacred to pilgrimage, and as such forbidden for the use of arms. To disarm suspicion, Abdallah's party shaved their heads, thus making the convoy believe that they had just returned from pilgrimage; and so these, falling into the trap, turned adrift their camels and began to cook their food. Meanwhile the Moslems, caught in a dilemma, debated what they should do:—"If we put off the attack," they said, "till the morrow, these men will cross the boundary, and find asylum in the sacred territory; if we attack them this night, it will be a transgression of the sacred month." As they argued thus, the Gordian knot was cut, for one drew his bow and shot dead a man of the unsuspecting band. On this, they rushed upon the caravan. One of the convoy escaped to Mecca. The remaining two were seized, and with the spoil carried off to Medina. Mahomet was displeased; and, saying that he had never bidden them to fight in the forbidden month, put the booty aside. Abdallah and his men were crestfallen, and the people reproached them. But not many days after, a revelation appeared justifying Sura ii. 217.
the act. "Warring in the sacred months," it said, "is grievous; but to deny God, and to expel His servants from their homes, is the greater sin." Having promulgated this dispensation, Mahomet made the booty over to the captors; and he also accepted a heavy ransom

for the prisoners, whose friends by this time had appeared to claim them.

The breach widens.

The native biographers rightly attribute much importance to this affair. "It was the first booty," says one, "that the Moslems captured; the first prisoners they seized; the first life they took." The breach was widening. No hostile response came at the moment from Mecca. But blood had been shed without the shadow of right; foully and sacrilegiously shed. And in Arabia, blood can be expiated by blood alone. At Medina, the coming struggle was steadily kept in view, as one of life and death, and began openly to be spoken of as such by Mahomet and his followers. The portions of the Coran revealed at this period abound with exhortations "to fight in the ways of the Lord," and to contribute towards the charges of the same. The oracle becomes the vehicle for many warlike utterances such as these:—

Fighting commanded in the Coran.

Sura xxii. 41.

Bear good tidings to the Righteous! Permission is given to bear arms against those that have wronged them, and have driven them from their homes for no other cause than this their saying, that *The Lord, He is our God.* And He will surely succour them that succour Him.

Sura ii. 191.

Fight on until Idolatry cease, and the Religion be God's alone. War is ordained, even if it be irksome unto you. Perchance, ye may dislike that which is good for you, and love that which is evil for you. But the Lord knoweth, and ye know not.

And again somewhat later:—

Prepare against them what force ye can, and troops of horse of your ability, that ye may thereby strike terror into the enemy of God and your enemy. And what thing soever ye contribute in the cause of God, it shall be made good unto you again.

Who is he that lendeth unto the Lord a goodly loan? He shall receive double for the same, and have an honourable recompense.

The command addressed equally to citizens of Medina.

Such passages are addressed not to the Refugees only, but to all believers, including the citizens of Medina. The first occasion on which these came forward in large numbers and warlike array was on the march to Bedr, and then probably with the hope of sharing in the spoil of a richly-laden caravan, rather than with the view of fighting for the faith and avenging the exiles' wrongs. But the effect was equally important to Mahomet. It pledged them to his cause.

CHAPTER XV.

BATTLE OF BEDR. JANUARY 624 A.D. A.H. II.

THE caravan of Abu Sofiân, already mentioned, would in ordinary course return from Syria in two or three months. Mahomet was resolved that it should not, like the others, slip through his hands. He gained over the tribes between Medina and the sea-shore to his project; and he sent two scouts to Haurân, on the Syrian road beyond Yenbo, to hasten back with tidings the moment the caravan approached. Mahomet had not yet learned to mask his movements; and so rumours of the intended attack reached Abu Sofiân while yet at a distance. He was greatly alarmed, and despatched Dhamdham with a message to the Coreish to hasten with an army to his rescue. Then he quickened his pace, taking the caravan by the route nearest the sea.

Designs against the caravan of Abu Sofiân.

Time passed, and the spies delaying their return, Mahomet became impatient. He resolved on immediate action; and thus addressed the people:—"See! here cometh a caravan in which the Coreish have embarked much wealth. Come! let us go forth; peradventure the Lord will enrich us with the same." The tempting call was eagerly responded to both by Refugees and Citizens. They marched three hundred and five in number, of

Mahomet sets out with an army, Jan 8, 623 A.D.

whom fourscore were Refugees. They had only two horses; but there were seventy camels, on which they rode by turns. The object was to strike the coasting road from Syria at the halting stage of Bedr, and there await the coming up of Abu Sofiân. Two scouts were sent forward, who were told by the women at the wells of Bedr that the caravan was expected in a day or two. They returned in haste to urge the little army on.

Abu Sofiân escapes with the caravan.

Meanwhile the apprehensions of Abu Sofiân were quickened as he approached the dangerous vicinity, and he hastened in advance of his caravan to reconnoitre. Reaching Bedr, he heard of the two spies, and going straightway to the wells, spied out the spot. "Camels of Yathreb!" he cried, as he saw among the refuse the peculiar stone of the Medina date; "these be the spies of Mahomet!" With these words, he hurried back to his people, and quickening the pace of the caravan, struck to the right, hugging the sea-shore: and so, halting neither day nor night, was soon beyond the reach of danger. Then, learning that an army had set out for his rescue, he sent on a courier to Mecca, saying that all being now safe, they might dismiss their apprehensions for the caravan and return home.

The Coreish march from Mecca.

We now turn back to Mecca, to see what had been passing there. Dhamdham, urging his camel through the city in hot haste, reached the Káaba, and there making it kneel, alighted, cut off the camel's ears and slashed its nose, in token of the pressing nature of his errand. Then reversing the saddle, he rent his clothes and shouted, "Coreish! O Coreish; your caravan is pursued by Mahomet. Help, O help!" At once the city was in a stir; for almost every one had a venture with Abu Sofiân. "Let us march," they cried, "to his succour with all speed. Doth Mahomet think to repeat the affair of Nakhla? Never! he shall know it otherwise." So moved was the spirit of Mecca that within two or three days—about the very time, in fact, that Mahomet was leaving Medina—the army marched from Mecca. They went in haste, but not without some rude display; for a company of singing-women followed, and sang martial songs by the fountains at which they halted. They were already half way to Bedr when the messenger of Abu Sofiân (who with his caravan had passed unnoticed by a route closer to the sea) brought the welcome news that all was safe. Should they retrace their steps, the object of their expedition being now secured, or still march on for their revenge? The matter was hotly debated. Warlike counsels and the memory of Nakhla at last prevailed. "If we go back," they said, "they will call us cowards. Let us go on to Bedr. There by its fountains we shall spend three days, eating and drinking. Arabia shall hear of it, and stand in awe." A few returned to Mecca, but the main body pursued its march.

Coreish march on Bedr.

Mahomet also was advancing rapidly on Bedr. From the accounts still coming in he believed the caravan to be behind, and expected to intercept it passing by. On the fifth day, while approaching Bedr, the startling news came that a great army was in full march to the help of Abu Sofiân. A council was summoned. With one voice all demanded an advance. The men of Medina vied with the Refugees. "Prophet of the Lord!" was their cry; "march on. By Him who hath sent thee with the Truth, we swear that if thou travellest till our

Mahomet too advances on Bedr.

Council of war.

camels fall down with fatigue, we shall go forward with thee to the world's end." "Then," replied Mahomet, "go forward with the blessing of the Lord. For verily He hath promised me one of the two,—the army or the caravan,—that He will deliver it into my hands. By the Lord! methinks that even now I see the battle-field strewn with their dead."

On nearing Bedr, Mahomet sent Aly forward with a party to reconnoitre. Two of the enemy, filling their skins at the wells, fell into their hands. Expecting to get intelligence from them of the caravan, they fell to beating these two captives, when Mahomet, coming up, drew from them the fact that the enemy was close at hand. He learned, moreover, that they were about a thousand strong—more than three-fold his own little army—mounted also on seven hundred camels, with a hundred horsemen all clad in mail. The Moslems were chagrined at the prospect of a rich and easy prey turned into that of a bloody battle. They still, indeed, seem to have hoped that a victory would enable them to pursue and seize the caravan. But it was better for them that it had passed, for a sense of its jeopardy would have nerved the enemy, and united them by a bond which its safety had already dissipated. A tiny rivulet from the eastern hills ran through the sandy valley, breaking out here and there into springs, which at various spots were dug into cisterns for the use of travellers halting there. The Moslems at once occupied the largest of these, and destroyed the rest.

Ground occupied at Bedr.

A hut of palm-branches was hastily run up, in which Mahomet and Abu Bekr passed the night. The army, wearied with the march, enjoyed

Mahomet retires to a hut.

refreshing sleep—a mark (we are told) of Divine interposition. As day dawned, the prophet rose betimes, drew out his little army, and placed a leader over each of the three companies,—the Beni Aus, the Beni Khazraj, and the Refugees.

Coreish advance in order of battle.

The Coreish too were busy marshalling their forces. But doubt and dissension again broke out in their ranks. One of their chiefs having made a reconnaissance of the enemy returned, saying: "Their numbers are small, but death is astride their camels. Their only refuge is the sword. Silent as the grave, they put forth their fangs with the serpent's deadly aim. For every man we slay, one of ourselves will fall, and what worth will life be after that?" The words began to tell, when Abu Jahl taunted his comrades with cowardice, and bade the brother of him that was slain at Nakhla to call his brother's blood to mind. Forthwith this man rent his clothes, cast dust upon his head, and began frantically to cry aloud his brother's name. The spirit spread, and thoughts of peace now scattered to the winds, all were eager to advance. The leaders bore three standards aloft, and guided thus the Coreish moved slowly forward across the sandy hillocks that separated them from their enemy. Facing eastwards, the rising sun was in their eyes, a serious drawback that told in favour of the Moslem side.

Anxiety of Mahomet. His prayer.

Mahomet had barely arranged the line of battle, when the advanced column of the Coreish appeared over the rising sand-hills in front. Their superior numbers were concealed by the fall of the ground behind.[1] But Mahomet knew the disparity

[1] This effect is in the Coran attributed to the direct interposition of God:—"And when He caused the enemy to appear in

of his little army, and, alive to the issue that hung upon the day, retired for a moment with Abu Bekr to his hut. Raising his hands aloft, he thus poured out his soul: "O Lord! if this little band be vanquished, Idolatry will again be rampant, and the pure worship of Thee cease from off the land." "The Lord," rejoined his friend, "will surely come to thine aid, and lighten thy face with the joy of victory."

Mahomet again came forth. The enemy was close at hand, but the Moslems kept still. They were not to stir till the prophet gave command; only, if their flank were threatened by the cavalry, they were to check the movement by a discharge of archery. The cistern was guarded as their palladium. Some desperate warriors of the Coreish swore that they would drink therefrom or perish in the attempt. But they were met by equal daring, and hardly one escaped alive the fatal enterprise. Already, after Arab fashion, single combats were being fought at various points along the line, when Sheyba and Otba, two leaders of the Coreish, and Welîd, son of Otba, still smarting under the taunts of Abu Jahl, advanced into the open field and defied three champions from the Medina force to meet them singly. Many upstarted at the call, but Mahomet checked them, and turning to his kinsmen said: "Ye sons of Hâshim! arise and fight, according to your right." Hamza, Obeida, and Aly, the uncle and cousins of Mahomet, stepped forth. Their features being concealed by their helmets, Otba asked their names. "Speak," he said, "and if ye be our

The battle of Bedr. 13th Jan. A.D. 624.

your eyes few in number."—Sura viii. The same Divine help is ascribed likewise to the rain, &c., as will be seen from a passage quoted further on.

equals we shall fight with you." Hamza answered, with a play on his name: "I am the *Lion* of God and of His prophet; I am the son of Abdal Mottalib." "A worthy foe," replied Otba; "but who are these?" Hamza gave their names. "Meet foes every one," replied Otba; and then they arose to fight. First, the two youngest, Welîd and Aly, rushed at each other. The combat was short and sharp. Welîd fell mortally wounded by the sword of Aly. Eager to avenge his son's death, Otba hastened forward, and Hamza stepped out to meet him. Swords gleamed quick, and again the Coreishite warrior fell, slain this time by the Moslem "lion." Sheyba remained the last; and Obeida, a veteran threescore years and five, drew near to fight with him. The conflict was this time less decisive. Sheyba dealt a blow which severed the tendon of Obeida's leg, and brought him to the ground. At this, Hamza and Aly rushed on Sheyba and despatched him with their swords.

The armies close.

The fate of their champions was ominous for the Coreish, and their spirit sank within them. The ranks closed with the battle-cry from the Moslem side, YÂ MANSÛR AMIT, *Ye conquerors, strike!* But there were still many scenes of individual heroism, such as are common in the irregular warfare of the East, and impart an Homeric interest to the page. Prodigies of valour were shown on both hands, but the army of Medina was borne along by an enthusiasm which the half-hearted warriors on the opposite side could not withstand. Tradition revels in the details. Thus we are told of Omeir, a stripling of sixteen, casting away a handful of dates he was eating: "Is it these," he cried; "that hold me back from Paradise? Verily I will taste no more of them until I meet my Lord!" And so, rushing on the enemy, he obtained the fate he coveted. A like ardour inspired the whole Moslem host.

It was a stormy day. A piercing blast swept across the valley. *That*, cried Mahomet, *is Gabriel with a thousand angels charging down upon the foe!* Another, and yet another blast; it was Michael and Serafîl, each with a like angelic troop. As the battle raged, the prophet stooped, and gathering a handful of gravel, cast it at the enemy, shouting, *Confusion seize their faces!* Just then came the turn of the tide. The thousand men of Mecca wavered before the onset of the brave three hundred, and gave way. The Moslems pursued their retreating steps, slaying or taking captive all that fell within their reach. Defeat soon turned into ignominious rout. The fugitive host, throwing away their heavy armour, abandoned camp and beasts of burden. Forty-nine were killed, and a like number taken prisoners. The army of Medina lost only fourteen, half of the number Citizens and half Refugees. Amongst the enemy's slain were some of the foremost chiefs, as well as some of Mahomet's bitterest opponents. Abu Jahl, his arch-enemy, lay yet breathing, when Abdallah cut off his head and cast it gory at his master's feet. "God! there is none other!" exclaimed Mahomet: "the head of His enemy is better to me than the best camel in all Arabia!"

Army of Mecca put to flight.

Abu Jahl killed.

When the enemy all were gone, the Moslems spent some time in gathering the booty. Then, as the sun declined, they dug a pit on the battle-field, and cast the enemy's dead into it. Mahomet stood by. "Otba, Sheyba, Abu Jahl," he cried exultingly, as one by one the bodies were thrown into the

Enemy's dead cast into a pit.

common grave; "have ye now found true that which your Lord did promise you? What my Lord promised me, that verily have I found to be true. Woe unto the people which rejecteth their prophet!" "Art thou talking with the dead?" asked a bystander. "Yea verily," spake Mahomet in reply, "for now they well know that the promise of their Lord hath fully come to pass."

Distribution of the booty.

Carrying their dead and wounded with them, the little army retired from the field of battle and passed the night in a valley some miles on the way home. A difference sprang up amongst them about the division of the booty,—some, as having been much to the front, claiming more than others. The contention grew so sharp that Mahomet interposed with a message purporting to be from heaven.

Sura viii.

"They will ask thee," so it ran, "concerning the prey; *Say,* the prey is the Lord's and His prophet's. Wherefore, fear God, and be obedient unto His prophet, if ye be true believers,"—and so on. The booty was then placed under a prize agent, and distributed. All shared alike, excepting that horsemen obtained a treble portion, and every soldier retained the spoil taken from the person of any one slain by his own hand. To the lot of each fell a camel, or a leathern couch, or some such equivalent. Mahomet took as his own share the famous camel of Abu Jahl, and a sword known by the name of *Dzul Ficâr.* About the same time was promulgated the ordinance which assigns a Fifth to the Prophet and the State; and this, with the precedent of equal distribution now established, is the Mussulman law of prize followed to the present day.[1]

[1] "Know that whatsoever spoil ye take, the Fifth thereof is for

From the field of battle, Mahomet despatched Zeid on Al Caswa to make known the victory at Medina. The disaffected citizens had buoyed themselves with the hope of Mahomet's defeat, and, seeing his favourite camel approach without its master, prognosticated that he was slain. But they were soon undeceived, for Zeid, taking his stand at the entrance of the city, proclaimed the overthrow of the Coreish, and named the chief men slain or taken prisoners. The joy of the prophet's adherents was unbounded; and as the news ran from door to door, the children made the streets resound with the cry, *Abu Jahl the sinner is slain!* Next day Mahomet himself returned. His happiness was damped by the loss of his daughter Rockeya, to tend whose death-bed, Othmân alone of the Refugees had remained behind. A few months later, Mahomet gave to Othmân his only unbetrothed daughter, Omm Kolthûm, who was formerly married to a cousin at Mecca, but had been for some time separated from him.

News of victory, how received at Medina.

Return of Mahomet.

The prisoners were handcuffed and marched along with the army. On their way two were ordered to be executed. One ventured to ask why he was dealt with more rigorously than the rest. "Because," replied Mahomet, "of thine enmity

Two prisoners put to death.

God and for His prophet, and for him that is of kin to the prophet, and for the orphan, and the poor, and the wayfarer; if ye be they that believe in God, and in the Revelation sent down to Our servant on the Day of Discrimination (so the Battle of Bedr is called), the day on which the two armies met; and God is over all things mighty."—Sura viii.

The mounted soldier had three shares, one for himself and two for his horse.

to God and His prophet." "And my little girl," cried the captive in bitterness of soul, "who will take care of her?" "Hell-fire," answered the prophet, as the victim was hewn to the ground. "Wretch and persecutor!" he continued; "scorner of God, of His prophet, and of His word; I thank the Lord, who hath comforted mine eyes by thy death."

Rest well treated.

We are even told that it had been in contemplation to put the whole of the prisoners, some fifty in number, to death. Omar, with characteristic severity, urged this, while Abu Bekr pressed for mercy. In the end their lives were spared; for a message (so the story runs) was brought by Gabriel, leaving to Mahomet the choice of either slaying them or demanding a ransom,—but with this condition, that for every captive spared, a Moslem would be hereafter slain in battle; and to this condition the army, coveting the ransom, readily agreed.[1] Such is the tradition; but the only mention of the matter in the Coran is the following passage delivered shortly after the battle:—

Sura viii.

> It is not for a prophet to take prisoners until he hath inflicted a grievous wound upon his enemies on the earth. Ye seek after the good things of this life; but God seeketh after the life to come. . . . Unless a revelation from the Lord had come unto you, surely a grievous punishment had overtaken you for the ransom that ye took. But now enjoy of that which ye have gained whatever is lawful and good. And fear the Lord, for He is gracious and forgiving.
>
> O prophet! speak thus unto thy prisoners,—If God should know anything in your hearts which is good, He will give unto you better than that which ye have lost. He will pardon your offences, for He is forgiving and merciful.

---

[1] In accordance with this tradition, it is held that the seventy Moslems slain the following year at Ohod, were so slain, man for man, in fulfilment of this compromise.

And so, in accordance with this command, when the prisoners were brought into Medina, Mahomet enjoined his people to treat them with kindness and consideration. "Blessings on the men of Medina!" said one of these in after days:—"they made us ride while they themselves walked afoot, and they gave us bread to eat when there was little of it, contenting themselves with dates." It is not surprising that some of the captives, yielding to these influences, declared themselves believers; and to such their liberty was at once granted. The rest were kept for ransom; but it was long before the Coreish could humble themselves to visit Medina for the purpose. At last they came, and the ransom was paid in large sums fixed according to their several means. Of such as had nothing to give, it was required that ten boys should be taught to write, and the teaching was accepted as a ransom.

Some embrace Islam. The rest ransomed.

The die was now cast. Mahomet had drawn the sword and thrown aside the scabbard. Having done so, there was little fresh risk to be incurred by making victory the test of his prophetic claim. However strong other arguments, his position could not be maintained in face of fatal reverse; however weak, conquest must in the end establish it. Therefore Mahomet was safe in ascribing his present success to the Divine aid, which he claimed to have been vouchsafed against superior force, and even against the machinations of the Devil. The following may be taken as a specimen of copious effusions to this effect:—

The victory ascribed to Divine aid.

When ye sought assistance from your Lord, and He answered, *Verily, I will assist you with a thousand angels in squadrons following one upon another;*—This the

Sura viii.

Lord did as good tidings for you, and to confirm your hearts thereby, for God is mighty and wise. When He overshadowed you with a deep sleep as a security from Himself, and caused it to rain that He might purify you withal, this was to confirm your hearts, and stablish your footsteps. . . .

And ye slew them not, but the Lord slew them. Neither was it thou, O prophet, that castedst the (handful of) gravel, but God did cast it. . . If ye desire a decision, now verily hath the Decision come unto you. . . Remember also when Satan bedecked their works unto the Enemy and said, *None shall prevail against you this day, for surely I am your Confederate.* But when the armies came within sight the one of the other, then Satan turned upon his heels, saying,—*I am clear of you; for verily I see that which ye see not. I fear God, for God is terrible in vengeance.*

Consternation at Mecca and thirst for revenge.

At Mecca, burning shame, and the thirst for revenge, stifled for a time all outward expression of grief. "Weep not for your slain," was the word passed round by Abu Sofiân; "neither let the bard bewail their fate. It will abate your wrath; and the foe will laugh at your lamentation. Haply the turn may come, and ye shall yet gain your revenge. As for me, I will touch no oil, neither come near my wife, until I shall have gone forth again to fight with Mahomet." A month of sullen restraint passed. Then the wild cry of long-stifled grief went up from Mecca. There was hardly a family in which wailing for the dead was not heard. One house was silent. "Why shed no tears?" they said to Hind, the wife of Abu Sofiân. "Why weep not for thy father Otba, thine uncle also, and thy brother?" She made answer: "I will not weep,—until war again be waged with Mahomet and his fellows. If tears could wipe the grief from off my heart, I too could weep. But it is not thus with Hind."

CHAPTER XVI.

ASSASSINATIONS AT MEDINA—EXPULSION OF A JEWISH TRIBE. A.H. III. A.D. 624. ÆTAT. 56.

Jews and disaffected citizens.

THE truimph at Bedr strengthened immeasurably the position of Mahomet at Medina. The consolidation of his power was followed by an early and decisive movement against the Jews and the Disaffected, who ventured still to raise their heads against him and gainsay his revelation.

Assassination of Asma, Jan. 624 A.D.

The first blood shed at Medina with the countenance of Mahomet was a woman's. Asma, daughter of Merwân, belonged to a family which still clung to the ancestral faith. She made no secret of her dislike to Islam, and being a poetess composed verses on the folly of putting faith in a Stranger who had risen against his own people and slain so many of them in battle. These verses quickly spread from mouth to mouth. The Moslems were offended, and Omeir, a blind man of the same tribe, and a former husband of the poetess, vowed that he would kill her. Tradition magnifies the assassin's merit by dwelling on his heartless cruelty. In the dead of night he crept to the apartment where Asma with her children lay asleep. Feeling stealthily, he removed her suckling babe, and plunging his sword into her breast, so transfixed her to the couch. Next morning, in the Mosque at prayer, Omeir acquainted Mahomet (who was aware of the design) with what he had done, and asked whether there was any cause for apprehension. "None whatever," replied the prophet; "a couple of goats will hardly knock their heads together for it." Then turning to the bystanders, he remarked, "Behold a man that hath assisted the Lord and His prophet." "What!" cried Omar, "the blind Omeir?" "Call him not blind," rejoined Mahomet; "call him rather Omeir the Seeing." On his way home Omeir encountered members of the family, who taxed him with the murder. He avowed it openly, and threatened the whole clan of them with the same fate unless they changed their tone. They were alarmed, and soon succumbed before the determined attitude of the Moslem party. In short, the only alternative to a hopeless blood-feud was now the adoption of Islam.

A few weeks later another foul murder was committed on Abu Afak, an aged Jewish proselyte, whose offence was similar to that of Asma. "Who will rid me of this pestilent fellow?" said Mahomet to those about him; and not long after, one of his followers fell unawares on the unfortunate man as he slept in his courtyard, despatched him with his sword, and escaped unrecognized. Horror at his death-shriek seized the Jews. There was good reason for it.

Another assassination, Feb. 624 A.D.

The Beni Cainucâa, one of the three Jewish tribes, followed the goldsmiths' craft in their stronghold outside the city. Shortly after his return from Bedr, Mahomet visited them there, and summoned them to acknowledge him as the Apostle of God, lest that should overtake them which at Bedr had

Beni Cainucâa attacked, Feb. 624 A.D.

befallen the Coreish. They refused, and defied him to do his worst. Pretext for attack soon offered. A Moslem maiden visited their market-place, and sat down at a goldsmith's, waiting for some ornaments. At her back, unperceived, a foolish neighbour pinned her skirt to the upper dress. When she arose there was laughter at the exposure, and she screamed with shame. A Mussulman hearing of it slew the Jew, and the Jews again fell upon the Mussulman and killed him. The family of the latter appealed to their fellows in Medina, who espoused their cause. Mahomet made no attempt to compose the quarrel or single out the guilty. Forthwith he marshalled his followers, and placing the great white banner, fresh from the field of Bedr, in the hands of Hamza, marched forth to attack the offending tribe. The settlement was too strong to carry by assault. It was therefore surrounded, a strict blockade maintained, and thus for fifteen days the siege was pressed. The beleaguered garrison expected relief from their allies, Abdallah ibn Obey, and his tribe the Beni Khazraj, but none dared stir on their behalf. At last they surrendered in despair. One by one they issued from the stronghold and were pinioned for execution. Abdallah could not bear the sight. Addressing himself to Mahomet, he begged for mercy, but Mahomet turned away. Then seizing him by the arm as he stood accoutred in his coat of mail, Abdallah reiterated his request. "Let me alone!" said Mahomet. But Abdallah did not relax his grasp. "Wretch, let me go!" cried the prophet, as anger mantled in his face. "Nay," answered Abdallah, "I will not let thee go until thou showest mercy on my friends—three hundred armed in mail and four hundred unequipped—who have stood by me on the field of battle. Wilt thou cut them down in one day?"

And sent into exile.

"Then let them go," said Mahomet sullenly. "The Lord curse them, and him too!" They were set at liberty and sent in exile to the north, where eventually they settled in the land of Syria. From the spoil, chiefly armour and goldsmiths' tools, Mahomet chose for himself some bows and swords and two coats of mail. The royal Fifth was set aside, and the rest distributed among the army.

Assassination of Kab son of Ashraf, July 624 A.D.

A few months passed, and another dastardly assassination darkens the page of the prophet's life. Kab ibn Ashraf, son of a Jewess, was a "proselyte of the Gate." He followed Mahomet so long as he favoured Judaism, but left him when he forsook Jerusalem as his Kibla. Mortified at the success of the new cause and the rejection of his faith, he visited Mecca, and there recited elogies extolling the heroes slain at Bedr, and stirring up the Coreish to avenge their death. Returning to Medina, he disquieted the Moslems by amatory verses addressed to their wives—a favourite mode of annoyance with the Arabs. Mahomet was greatly displeased, and made no secret of his animosity. "O Lord," he prayed aloud, "rid me of the son of Ashraf in whatsoever way Thou wilt, because of his sedition and his evil verses." And he prompted his followers to the deed, saying, "Who will ease me of this pestilent fellow? for he troubleth me." Mohammed son of Maslama came forward. "Here am I," he said; "I will slay him." Four others joined him, and the plot was soon matured. Kab was thrown off his guard by the demand of a loan, and an hour was appointed in the dead of night, when the conspirators were to lodge their arms, as security for repayment, at his house in an outlying suburb. Mahomet accompanied them to the outskirts of the town, and as they went on their deed of darkness bade them God-speed. Caught in the snare, and not startled by their arms, Kab descended at their call; when, decoying him to a distance, they despatched him with their swords. Escaping pursuit, they hurried back, carrying one of their number severely wounded in the struggle. As they entered the gateway of the Mosque, Mahomet met them. "Welcome!" he exclaimed; "for I see that your faces beam with victory." "And thine too!" they added, as they cast the ghastly head of their victim at his feet. Tradition dwells with complacency on the aggravating details of this perfidious murder; and the stigma of complicity in the same cannot be dissociated from the prophet's name.

Disquietude of the Jews.

Another murder soon followed, and threats of yet more. Exasperated at the opposition (tradition terms it the treachery) of the stiff-necked Jews, Mahomet gave his followers permission to slay them at discretion. The Jews were thrown into great alarm. None ventured abroad, for fear of assassination. At last a deputation waited on the prophet, and complained of his hostile attitude, and specially of the treacherous end of Kab. "Had he behaved himself," answered Mahomet, "as ye have done, he would not have thus been put to death; but he vexed me by his evil speech and verse; and if ye do the same, ye too shall in like manner be cut off." At the same time he invited them to enter into a fresh treaty of friendship, which they did. Nevertheless (tradition adds) the Jews henceforward lived, as well they might, in much depression and disquietude.

Raid on Medina by Abu Sofiân.

During this year, the Third at Medina, martial spirit was kept on the alert by several warlike passages, though none were of any marked importance. In the spring Abu Sofiân, smarting under the defeat of Bedr, vowed that he would carry fire and sword into the city of his enemy. With two hundred followers he succeeded, with the connivance of certain chief men of the Jews, in effecting a raid upon the suburbs, burning some farms and killing the cultivators. Then, considering his vow fulfilled, he beat a hasty retreat before the alarm could be given in the town.

Expeditions in Nejd.

The route to Syria by the sea-shore being now barred to the Coreish, they began to send their caravans across the peninsula to Irâc. Repeated expeditions were accordingly planned by Mahomet against those Bedouin tribes in Nejd which took the Meccan side, especially the Beni Suleim and Ghatafân who acted as carriers to the Coreish. In the autumn a lucky dash was made on one of these ventures while in transit towards the head of the Persian Gulf, by Zeid with one hundred mounted men. The convoy fled, and large spoils in vessels and bars of silver were taken, so that eight hundred dirhems fell to each man's lot. This was the first occasion on which the Moslems secured rich plunder from a caravan.

Caravan captured.

Mahomet marries Haphsa, Nov. 624 A.D. A.H. III.

In this year Mahomet took to himself a third wife, Haphsa, daughter of Omar, then about twenty years of age. She was the widow of an early convert, recently deceased. Omar and Abu Bekr were thus both similarly connected with the prophet. There was much rivalry between Ayesha and Haphsa, but Ayesha succeeded in maintaining her supremacy.

The marriages contracted by Mahomet at Medina were all unfruitful, and no issue of his elder daughter survived. It was through the youngest, Fâtima, that the prophet's race was to be perpetuated. Being now seventeen years of age, her father gave her in marriage to Aly, who was five-and-twenty, and who, as we have seen, had already distinguished himself on the field of Bedr. Within the next twelve months she gave birth to Hasan, and the year after to Hosein,—names famous in Islam.

Marriage of Fâtima with Aly, 624 A.D.

CHAPTER XVII.

BATTLE OF OHOD. JANUARY 625 A.D. A.H. III.

Tidings of intended attack on Medina.

THE Third year of Mahomet's life at Medina had nearly closed, and the winter had again set in, when a storm clouded the horizon. Twelve months had passed since the battle of Bedr, and the cry for revenge still resounded in the vale of Mecca. Rumours of a threatened attack had for some time prevailed at Medina, when a sealed epistle was put into the hands of Mahomet. Hastily despatched by Abbâs, who still retained a kindly interest in his nephew, it carried the startling news that a great army was on the point of marching on the city. Mahomet enjoined secrecy, but the matter soon oozed out, and caused much excitement, especially amongst the Jews and the disaffected citizens. There was cause for alarm. The merchandise brought back to Mecca by the luckless caravan, for which so much blood had been shed, was stored up hard by the Káaba, and there had lain ever since, untouched. The profits of the fatal venture were now, by general consent, devoted to the equipment of an avenging force. The Bedcuin allies of the desert were invited to join the enterprise. The army marched three thousand strong.

Coreish march from Mecca, Jan. 625 A.D. A.H. III.

Seven hundred were clad in mail, two hundred were mounted on horses, the remainder rode on camels. Fifteen women followed in the train, and, taking timbrels in their hands, sang to their wild cadence songs of vengeance for kinsmen slain at Bedr. Foremost was Hind, wife of Abu Sofiân, who, thirsting for the blood of Hamza, the slayer of her father, had engaged an Ethiopian warrior to make the surer of her victim. They took the ordinary route till they drew nigh to Medina, when they fetched a circuit to the left, and then turning northward encamped in a fertile plain beneath the hill of Ohod. The corn was cut for forage, and the camels, set loose to graze, trampled down the rich fields around. Between the city and the plain were several rocky ridges which guarded the way against direct attack. The high road from Syria, avoiding these, swept eastward from under Ohod, and reached the city by an easy circuit. The Coreish feared to advance by this road, because the houses on that approach would have afforded their adversaries a position of dangerous offence. They hoped rather to draw them forth, and overpower them by their numbers upon equal ground. Perhaps also they expected by delay to create some dangerous diversion in the city.

And encamp near Medina.

Meanwhile Mahomet by his spies was kept aware of the movements of the enemy. The farmers, with their cattle and their stuff, had effected a timely retreat, but the destruction of their fields was a trial sore to bear. Still, there was no ebullition of feeling against Mahomet as the cause of all this misfortune. Indeed, so great was the hold he had already gained upon the people, that he was at once

Resolution of Mahomet to remain within the city;

recognized as the proper defender of the city. An armed company of citizens kept watch throughout the night by his door. He dreamed, we are told, a dream in his troubled sleep. Clad in impenetrable armour, he rode upon a ram, when suddenly the sword was broken in his hand, and a steer was slaughtered in his sight. Next day a council of the town was called, and before them all he thus interpreted the dream. "The broken sword," he said, "portendeth some injury to myself; the slaughter of the steer some damage to the people; riding on the ram signifieth carnage among the enemy; and the impenetrable coat of mail is Medina, fortified and safe. Here remain, we are secure. Go forth, and there is risk and danger!" The men of years agreed; Abdallah ibn Obey, equally concerned in the defence, concurred. "The city," he said, "is a virgin inviolate; quitting the city, we have ever suffered loss; staying within it, we have beaten back attack. Leave the Coreish alone. If they remain, it will be in evil case; at length, frustrated in their attempt, they will retire." It was resolved accordingly to bring all outlying inhabitants within the walls, and, if the Coreish should venture near, to drive them back by a galling discharge of arrows and stones from the walls and house-tops.

Set aside, to satisfy younger followers.

The decision displeased the younger citizens. "Shall we sit at home," they cried, "a laughing-stock to all Arabia, and look quietly on while our goods before our very eyes are ravaged everywhere around? Nay, we will go forth and smite the enemy, even as we did at Bedr." Their importunity was so great that, against his better judgment, Mahomet at the last gave way, and announced his readiness to offer battle to the enemy. Ascending the pulpit after the Friday service, he stirred up the people to fight courageously. "And if ye be steadfast," he added, "the Lord will give you the victory." While they were mustering with their arms in the courts of the Mosque, Mahomet retired to make ready. After a little he issued forth, clad in mail and helmet, his sword hanging from his girdle, and shield slung over his shoulder. The citizens, seeing him thus accoutred, repented of their rash remonstrance, and bade him even now to do as it seemed best to him. But it was too late. "I invited you to this," he said, "and ye would not. It becometh not a prophet, when once he hath girded himself to the battle, to lay his armour down until that the Lord hath decided betwixt him and his enemy. Only be steadfast, and the Lord will surely send you victory."

Mahomet marches forth to Ohod.

So saying he placed three banners in the hands of the three separate bands,—the Refugees, the Beni Aus, and the Beni Khazraj, and mounting his horse, led the way to Ohod. There was but one other horse with the Moslem army. On the road Mahomet saw, drawn up amongst the palm groves, a disorderly band of fighting men, and being told that they were the Jewish confederates of Abdallah, he ordered them back; "for," said he, "ye shall not this day seek help of unbelievers to fight against the unbelieving." Half-way the army halted for the night. Vigilant patrol was kept up on either side, and though the armies were separated by a ridge, the Coreish came close enough to alarm the Moslems by the neighing of their horses. At dawn the army of Medina, a thousand strong, was in motion. They crossed the intervening fields, and emerged upon the sandy plain beneath the hill of Ohod. By this time it was daylight, and although the enemy was in sight, the hour for worship having come, Bilâl raised the well-known cry, and the army prostrated itself in prayer. Just then Abdallah, who had not got over the unfriendly treatment of his Jewish allies, deserted with three hundred followers, and took the road back to Medina. Mahomet was thus left with but seven hundred men, of whom only one hundred were clad in mail; while, face to face, was a well-appointed enemy, four times the number. Reaching the skirt of the hill, they halted, having behind them and on their right the frowning rocks of Ohod. On their left was open ground; and here, as a protection against the Coreishite horse, Mahomet posted on an eminence the flower of his archery, with stringent orders to guard the flank, and on no possible contingency to quit the spot. Then he drew out the line of battle, with the Refugees in the centre, and the Beni Aus and Khazraj on either wing. Having thus disposed his force, and forbade them till the word was given to stir, he put on a second coat of mail, and calmly awaited the enemy's advance.

Battle opens with single combats, 26 Jan. 624.

The army of Mecca, marshalled by Abu Sofiân, the hereditary leader, soon came up. The right wing was led by Khâlid, the left by Ikrima son of Abu Jahl, and the horse by Amru. The women at first kept to the front, and beat their timbrels to shrill martial song, but as the line advanced they fell to the rear. According to custom, the battle opened with single combats, and here the Coreish fared badly as they encountered the reckless daring of the Moslem champions. Their standard-bearer fell by the sword of Aly; and his son and brothers, five in number, one after another, striving to uphold the banner, met the same fate. The women beat their timbrels wildly, but in vain. At this opening stage their superior numbers gave the Meccans no advantage. At last the engagement became general; and here again the fierce ardour of the Medina army at the first carried all before it. The same heroism was shown, and contempt of danger, as at Bedr. Abu Dojâna, winding a red kerchief about his helmet, swept along the enemy's ranks, dealing death at every hand. Aly, conspicuous afar off by his long white plume, Hamza, known by a waving ostrich feather, and Zobeir by his bright yellow turban, like heroes in the war of Troy, carried confusion wherever they appeared. The Meccan army, thus pressed, began, despite its numbers, to waver. But now the Moslems pursued too hotly their success. Their line lost shape and order. A column piercing through the enemy's ranks fell to plundering his camp. The band of bow-men, whose galling archery had hitherto held the Meccan horse in check, saw from their eminence the tempting opportunity, and casting the prophet's strict injunction to the winds, hurried off to the spoil. The quick eye of Khâlid perceived the chance. Wheeling his cavalry round the Moslem left, and sweeping from the height the few remaining archers, he charged into his enemy. The surprise was fatal and the discomfiture complete. The standard-bearer of the Refugees was slain, and his banner disappeared. Hind's wild negro, who had been watching for Hamza, now singled out his victim, and swinging his javelin with unerring aim, brought him lifeless to the ground. The Moslems broke at every point, and fled for refuge to the overhanging rocks of Ohod.

Engagement becomes general.

Khâlid's generalship.

The Moslems routed.

Mahomet wounded.

It was a moment of peril for Mahomet. He was still in the rear, watching from a rising ground the first success, when he narrowly escaped the sweeping charge of Khâlid. Then he tried to check the flight. "Whither away?" he cried. "Come back! The Apostle of God is here. Come back!" But still they fled. Just then the enemy bore down upon him, and if a party of devoted followers had not rallied round the spot, he surely had been slain. Stones and arrows flew thick about him. A missile wounded his lip and broke one of his teeth. Another blow drove the rings of his helmet into his cheek, and made a gash in his forehead. A sword flourishing over his head was barely warded off by Talha, whose hand was thereby disabled for life. The cry went up that the prophet was slain, and it spread consternation among his followers. "Where was now," they asked one of the other, "the promise of his Lord?" The same cry, however, had this advantage for the Moslems, that, taken up in the enemy's ranks, it had the immediate effect there of staying pursuit. If Mahomet were dead, their object was fulfilled.

Finds refuge on the hill.

But Mahomet was only stunned. The faithful band around him hastened to make him climb the cliffs behind, whither the most of the army had already fled. A cave is still pointed out in which the prophet is said to have taken shelter. As he rested here they removed his helmet, and found two of the rings so deeply imbedded in his cheek that Abu Obeida lost two of his teeth in the attempt to draw them out. Then they fetched water from an adjoining spring to rinse his mouth and wash his face. As they did so Mahomet cursed the evil-doers "who had besprinkled the countenance of their prophet with his own blood." But soon recovering equanimity, he joined the rest of his followers, some of whom wearied with the struggle had fallen asleep, and watched thus the movements of the Coreish in the plain below. These sought for the body of Mahomet on the field of battle, and not finding it, began to doubt his death.

Many acts of barbarous mutilation were in the interval done upon the slain. Hind gloated over the corpse of Hamza, and tearing out his liver, fulfilled her savage vow in chewing it. Having buried his dead, Abu Sofiân drew near the foot of the hill and called aloud, "*Mahomet! Abu Bekr! Omar!*" Receiving no reply, for the prophet had enjoined silence, he cried again, "Then all are slain, and ye are rid of them." Omar could contain himself no longer. "Thou liest, enemy of God!" he exclaimed; "they are alive, and will repay thee yet." "Then," rejoined Abu Sofiân, "this day shall be a requital for Bedr. Ye will find mutilated ones upon the field; but it was not by my desire. Glory to Hobal! Glory to Ozza! *Ozza*[1] is ours!" Omar, prompted this time by the prophet, retorted, "The LORD is ours, and He is not yours." "We shall meet," said Abu Sofiân, "after a year, again at Bedr." With these words he turned to go, and the Meccan army began its homeward march.

Colloquy between Abu Sofiân and Omar.

When they were out of sight, Mahomet descended from his retreat. He found the plain strewn with the dead. Seventy lay slain on his own side, and but twenty on the enemy's. Medina too was in alarm. The Disaffected ill concealed their

Army of Mecca retires.

[1] Names of the two great idols at Mecca. There is a play on the word *ozza*, which signifies *glory*, as well as the great idol Ozza. He meant, "The glory rests with us."

feelings, and some even talked of an embassy to Abu Sofiân. The way taken by the Coreish branched off, at a little distance, in two directions, one leading direct to Medina, the other towards the shore. When they had reached this point the army paused. Some urged an attack upon the defenceless city; but in the breast of the greater number revenge was already sated, and so at last, wending their way through the defiles, they took the road to Mecca. Mahomet's spies hastened to him with the welcome news. "Gently," he said; "we must not seem before the people to rejoice at a departing enemy." The intelligence, nevertheless, was grateful both to Mahomet and to those about him; for the disabled, crestfallen army could ill have ventured on a second conflict.

Burial of dead.

The people of Medina now flocked to the field of battle, tending the wounded and searching for the dead. Among them was Fâtima, who dressed the gash on her father's head, staunching the blood with the ash of some matting. The wound was deep, and did not heal up for a month. "Where is my brother Hamza?" asked Safia eagerly of Mahomet. He would willingly have kept her from the sight, but she refused to go back. So he led her to the spot. She sat down with Fâtima by the body, and both wailed aloud. Mahomet wept also. His spirit was stirred within him at the sight of the mangled remains of the noble dead, and the anguish of his aunt. Pulling angrily at his beard, he swore that he would yet mutilate thirty corpses of the Coreish in revenge for that of Hamza (an oath, however, which he soon revoked); and he consoled his aunt by the assurance that her brother's name had already been enrolled in Paradise as *the Lion of God and of His Apostle.* He spoke comfortably also to the women of Medina, who had come out to wail over their dead. The graves being now ready, and the bodies laid out in order, he commanded them to be buried by twos and threes together. The obsequies ended, he mounted his horse, and the crowd, soldiers and citizens, turning sadly from Ohod, took the homeward road.

On the way, it being afternoon, the whole company, at Mahomet's command, fell into two lines, with the women behind, and offered up prayer to God. As they entered the city, the voice was heard all round of women wailing for their dead. "And Hamza!" exclaimed Mahomet; "alas for Hamza! Who is there to wail for Hamza?" The wounded were mostly carried to their homes. The rest followed Mahomet to the Mosque for evening service. It was a night of mourning. A sense of insecurity prevailed, for the Coreish might even yet return to the attack, and so the chief men again kept watch at the prophet's door. Some of the wounded were laid near the Mosque, and the fires kindled for them cast a fitful light about its courts. Mahomet slept heavily, and did not answer Bilâl's call for nightly prayer. Shortly after, awaking, he asked who those were that cried so pitifully hard by. It was the wailing of the women who had heard his plaintive words about Hamza, and had come together to mourn for him. And so it grew to be a custom at Medina, that the women, whenever they mourn for their dead, first raise a wail for Hamza.

Night of distress.

To raise the drooping spirits of his followers, Mahomet on the morrow gave orders for pursuing the enemy. Stiff and disfigured, he mounted his horse, and set out upon the Meccan road. But

Demonstration against enemy.

besides cutting up a few incautious stragglers, there was nothing done. After two or three marches, the prophet called a halt; and having kindled five hundred bonfires on the heights above, returned to Medina, contented with the demonstration. "Never again," he said to Talha, "shall the Coreish inflict a like humiliation on us; no, not till we shall wrest the Holy city from their hands."

A flood of glory surrounds the memories of the dead. Many years after, a torrent having ploughed up the valley, their bodies were said to have been seen reclining in the attitude of sleep, fresh and bleeding as on the day of interment. Mahomet was wont to visit the sacred spot once every year, and to pray, "Peace be on you for that which ye endured, and a blessed Futurity above!" The citizens, too, as they passed the spot would ejaculate, "*Peace be on you!*" and their fancy made it seem as if they caught the audible response, "*And on you be peace!*" Thus a halo in the course of time gathered around "the Martyrs of Ohod," and glorified their names. But at the present moment, shame, and not glory, overshadowed the battle-field. The people murmured at the disaster. Having already made victory an evidence of his mission, it required all the address of Mahomet to parry the converse argument based upon defeat. This was done by a message from heaven which now forms a part of the Third Sura. In it the prophet is reminded that the field of Bedr was won by the immediate interposition of the Almighty. The discomfiture at Ohod was needful to sift the faithful. These had coveted the martyr's crown, and lo, when it was brought nigh to them they turned on their heels and fled. Yet they

Halo around "Martyrs" of Ohod.

Defeat explained away in Coran.

fled in vain, for the hour of each is fixed and inevitable. Already the Lord had given victory, when cowardice and disobedience brought defeat. Even if Mahomet were slain,—what then? Apostles and prophets before him had gone the way of all flesh. He might die, but the cause would live, and in the end would truimph. Such is the argument, mingled with invective and rebuke, admonition and encouragement. Whatever the Disaffected might say of the prophet's doubtful logic, it served to reassure his loyal people, and while these were with him heart and soul, he had not much to fear.

Passages on the subject.

A few passages from this remarkable Sura will best show the reader the position taken up at this juncture by Mahomet, as well as illustrate the prosaic level to which his oracle had now subsided. It had come to be used not merely for the revelation of things Divine, but also as the vehicle for the promulgation of orders on the daily concerns of the commonwealth,—political, social, domestic, and personal,—and all couched in the same style as the messages direct from Deity.

Sura iii.

Remember when thou wentest forth from thy family in the early morning to prepare for the believers a camp for the battle, . . and when two companies of you became anxious,[1] so that ye lost heart. [Then follows the mention of Bedr and the angelic hosts that smote the enemy there.] Now, therefore, be not cast down, neither be ye grieved. Ye shall be again victorious, if ye indeed be faithful. Although a wound hath befallen you, surely a wound the like thereof hath already befallen your enemy. . .

What! did ye think that ye should enter Paradise while as yet the Lord had not proved them that were for Him? . . And truly

---

[1] Meaning the Beni Aus and Khazraj, forming the two wings, which were disconcerted when Abdallah deserted with his three hundred.

ye longed for death until ye faced it. . . Mahomet is no more than an apostle as other apostles were before him. What! if he were to die, or be slain, must ye therefore turn back upon your heels? . . And, verily, the Lord had already fulfilled His promise when with His help ye were slaying the enemy, until ye lost heart and were rebellious.[1] Then He turned you to flight from before them, that He might prove you; when ye fled to the mountain, and looked not back on any, although the apostle was calling unto you, even unto the hindermost amongst you. Wherefore He rewarded you with grief upon grief. And after the grief He sent down upon you peace,—even a soft slumber that overshadowed a part of you.[2] But others of you were troubled in their own souls, questioning about God that which is not the truth,—heathenish doubts,—in that they said, *Have we any ground of expectation at all in this concern?*[3] SAY, *Verily the concern appertaineth wholly unto the Lord.* They concealed in their heart that which they did not open unto Thee.. They said, *Had there been any ground of expectation for us in this concern, surely we had not here been slain.* SAY, Even had ye been in your own dwellings, verily those would have gone forth for whom fighting was ordained, unto the place of their death. . . Truly those amongst you who turned their backs on the day when the two armies met, Satan caused them to stumble for some wickedness which they had wrought. But the Lord hath forgiven them, for the Lord is forgiving and merciful.

Then he describes the blessed state of "the Martyrs" who fell in the battle:—

Think not in any wise of those slain in the ways of the Lord as if they were dead. Yea, they are alive, and nourished with their Lord,—exulting in that which He hath bestowed on them of His favour, and rejoicing on behalf of those that have not yet joined them, but are following after. Alarms affect them not, neither are they grieved.

Blessedness of the Martyrs.

---

[1] Meaning the disobedience of the archers, who deserted their post.

[2] Referring to those that slept after finding refuge on the mountain.

[3] That is, the expectation of Divine aid, such as had been promised by Mahomet.

CHAPTER XVIII.

TWO MISHAPS—EXPULSION OF THE BENI NADHIR.

A.D. 625. A.H. IV. ÆTAT. 57.

THE Coreish were satisfied with the punishment they had inflicted upon Mahomet. On returning from Ohod to Mecca, Abu Sofiân went straightway to the Káaba and rendered thanks to Hobal. Then he shaved his head and returned to his home, absolved from his vows of abstinence. Medina now enjoyed a long respite from the designs of Mecca. But the prestige of Mahomet had been seriously shaken amongst the Bedouin tribes, and these, emboldened by his late defeat, or it may be instigated by the Coreish, gave from time to time fresh trouble and anxiety. The early intelligence, however, which he secured by means of an effective espionage, enabled him to anticipate their movements, and generally to disperse their gatherings without serious loss. But there were exceptions.

Attitude of the Coreish and central tribes.

The centre of one of these hostile combinations was the Beni Lahyân, a tribe subservient to the Coreish; but their designs were anticipated by the assassination of their chief at the hand of an emissary from Medina. In revenge for this act of treachery, six of Mahomet's spies were attacked while

Mishap at Ra May 625. A.H. IV.

hovering near the tribe at Rajî, in the vicinity of Mecca. Four were slain. The two survivors were carried prisoners to Mecca, and sold to the families of certain chiefs who had fallen at Bedr. By them they were kept some time in confinement, and eventually taken beyond the limits of the sacred territory. There, before a great concourse from the city, they were cruelly put to death. The scene was memorable. The two martyrs—for such to the cause of Islam they really were—refused liberty offered them at the price of recantation. When bound to the stake they offered up prayer, and then cried loudly, "*Lord, number these men one by one, and destroy them; let not one escape!*" The multitude, thinking to avoid the potency of the curse, fell flat upon the ground. Then with daggers put into the hands of the children whose fathers had been killed at Bedr, they thus stabbed their victims. And so ended the wretched tragedy.

Two Moslem martyrs.

Shortly after, a more serious catastrophe took place. A company of seventy men was despatched by Mahomet to Nejd, with the view of bringing over the Beni Aamir to his cause. After four days' march they halted at the fountains of Bîr Maûna, and sent a letter to the chief, inviting the tribe to embrace Islam. Instead of accepting the call, this chief stirred up the Beni Suleim, a neighbouring tribe, which having lost relatives at Bedr was bitterly hostile, to attack the strangers. The band was surrounded and, excepting two, cut every one to pieces. The disaster, following so close on that of Rajî, greatly afflicted Mahomet. For a whole month at the morning service he invoked vengeance on the perpetrators of the outrage, saying, "*Lord, in Thine indignation trample under-*

Moslem party cut up at Bir Maûna.

foot the rebellious tribes" (naming them one by one), "*for that they have risen up against the Lord and against His prophet.*" He professed also to have received a heavenly message from the martyrs of Maûna, saying, "Acquaint our people that we have met our Lord; He is well pleased with us, and we with Him."

The tragedy of Maûna involved a still graver issue. One of the survivors on his way home fell in with two men of the guilty tribe, and slew them while asleep, by way of reprisal. But it turned out that these two men had just been to Medina, and there had obtained terms from Mahomet. The prophet, therefore, was displeased at the murder, and forwarded to the tribe the price of their blood. But the matter did not rest there. The Jewish tribe Beni Nadhîr were allies of the Beni Aamir, and Mahomet thought that as such they were bound to aid him in paying the blood-money; with this purpose he visited their stronghold. Having entered and sat down, they courteously invited him to a repast. While it was preparing, he rose abruptly, and leaving his companions seated, walked out of the assembly. Time passed, and as he did not return, his followers also arose and returned to the city. To their surprise, they found that Mahomet had gone back straightway to the Mosque, and there given out (so tradition runs) that the Jews had plotted to take his life by casting down from their roofs great stones upon him as he sat below. He had been warned, he said, of their treachery by a Divine monition. But as there is no mention of this in the Coran (which dwells at considerable length upon incidents connected with the siege), and there had been nothing to excite the suspicion of his followers, the story is somewhat

Beni Nadhîr ordered into exile, June 625 A.D. A.H. IV.

doubtful. However this may be, a message was forthwith despatched to the unfortunate tribe:—"*Thus saith the prophet of the Lord, Ye shall go forth from out of my land within ten days; whosoever after that remaineth behind shall be put to death.*" The message was received with dismay. The bearer of it was one of their old comrades, and they reproached him with being the carrier of such tidings to them. "*Hearts are changed,*" was his only answer, as he turned and left them.

They are besieged.

They hesitated. It was grievous to them to quit their fields and their groves, and the homes of their fathers. Their allies, the Beni Aus, were also touched with concern for their sad fate, and Abdallah ibn Obey strove in vain to bring about a reconciliation. Buoyed with the hope of aid from this quarter, as well as from the tribes in Nejd, and also by the strength of their fortress, they returned answer that they would not depart. "*Allah Akbar!*" exclaimed Mahomet, unable to conceal his delight; "*the Jews are going to fight. Great is the Lord!*" and the cry, taken up by his followers, resounded through the courts of the Mosque. Putting on their armour, they issued forth at once to invest the rebellious fortress. The besieged contrived by showers of stones and arrows from the battlements to keep their assailants at bay. But they looked in vain for succour. The Coreitza—now the only other Jewish tribe remaining—would not stir hand or foot on their behalf, though it might have been better for them at once to have perished on the field of battle, than thus reserve themselves for the worse fate which befel them two years later on. Still the Beni Nadhîr held out gallantly. Mahomet became impatient, and to hasten their departure resorted to an expedient deemed unlawful in Arab warfare. He began to cut down the surrounding clumps of palm trees and to burn their roots with fire. The Jews remonstrated against an act barbarous not only in itself, but specially forbidden by the Mosaic law; and Mahomet, sensible of the reproach, justified the act by an alleged Divine permission.

When the siege had now lasted some weeks, the garrison, seeing no prospect of relief, sent to say that they were ready to lay down their arms, abandon their ancestral lands, which now had lost to them their chief value, and leave the neighbourhood. Mahomet, fearing the danger to which, with disaffection still around, a protracted siege might expose him, accepted the terms and broke up his camp. The Beni Nadhîr then laded their property, even to the doors and lintels, upon camels, and with tabrets and music took the way to Syria. Some of them turned aside to the Jewish settlement of Kheibar; the rest went on to Jericho and the highlands of Judæa.

And sent in exile into Syria.

By a special revelation it was ordained that, there having been no actual fighting, the spoil should be distributed at the discretion of the prophet. It consisted, besides a great store of arms, in the fertile fields and palm-steads of the exiled tribe. A portion was kept by Mahomet for the support of his family and for the relief of the poor; the rest was distributed amongst the Refugees, who, thus endowed with valuable estates, were now in a position to dispense with the hospitality which had up to this time been so freely ministered by the Citizens of Medina. Two Jews of the exiled tribe, having embraced the dominant faith, were maintained in their possessions. Thus early were

Distribution of booty.

temporal inducements brought to bear on the aggrandisement of Islam.

A Sura devoted to the siege.

The expulsion of the Beni Nadhîr was a material triumph to Mahomet. One by one he was breaking up the Jewish settlements, and weakening the cause of disaffection within and without. An entire Sura is devoted to the short campaign. A few verses from it will illustrate the tenor of the oracle;—

Sura lix.

The Lord hath driven forth the unbelieving Jews from their habitations to join the former exiles. Ye thought not that they would go forth, and they thought that their Stronghold would defend them against God. But the Lord cast terror into their hearts. They pulled down their habitations with their own hands.

Whatsoever thou didst cut down of the Date trees, or left of them standing on their roots, it was done by the command of God, that He might abase the evil-doers. [Then follow instructions for distribution of the booty, with a eulogy of the Citizens who did not grudge their share in it to the Refugees, and also an invective against Abdallah ibn Obey and his followers.] Hast thou not observed the hypocrites? They say unto their brethren, the unbelieving Jews, *If ye be driven forth, verily we shall go forth with you, . . . and if ye be attacked, we shall surely help you.* But God is witness that they are liars. If they be attacked, these will not help them. They never will fight against you, saving from within fenced towns, or from behind walled places. . . . Ye think that they are united, but their hearts are parted asunder. . . .

Peroration on the Deity.

The Sura, catching (as the oracle every here and there still does) something of its early fire, closes with a splendid peroration:—

He is the Lord. Beside Him there is no God. It is He that knoweth both the Seen and the Unseen. The Merciful, the Compassionate. There is no God but He; the King, the Holy, the Giver of Peace, the Faithful, the Guardian, the Glorious, the Almighty, the Most High. Far exalted is the Lord above that which they associate Him with,—God, the Creator, the Maker, the Framer. Most goodly are His names. All that is in the heavens and in the earth praiseth Him. He is the Glorious, the Wise.

Zeid ibn Thâbit, amanuensis to Mahomet.

Hitherto Jewish amanuenses had been employed by Mahomet in writing out such despatches as were needed in the Syriac and Hebrew tongues. But he now saw good reason to distrust the people whom he had so deeply injured, and therefore commissioned a young Citizen, Zeid son of Thâbit, to undertake the duty. Zeid had already learned to read and write in Arabic from the prisoners taken at Bedr. He now qualified himself in the language of Syria, and was established in the post of Secretary. It is the same Zeid who was afterwards employed by the Caliphs in collecting the scattered fragments and Suras of the Coran into one volume.

CHAPTER XIX.

MARRIAGE WITH ZEINAB—OTHER DOMESTIC EVENTS.

A.D. 625, 626. A.H. IV., V. ÆTAT. 57, 58.

Bedr the Second. Spring, 625. A.H. IV.

FOR a time Medina was undisturbed by the hostile sound of arms. Occasional campaigns were undertaken against the tribes in the desert, but none of serious consequence. On the anniversary of Ohod the threatened combat at Bedr did not take place. A severe drought had burned up the provender throughout the land. Abu Sofiân did indeed march from Mecca with a great army, but he deemed the scarcity a reason sufficient for turning back. Mahomet, however, undeterred by exaggerated rumours caused by the preparations of the Coreishite force, kept his word, and reached the appointed place at the head of fifteen hundred men, double the number he had as yet led into the field. His followers also carried stores of merchandise for the yearly fair held there. They encamped for a week by the wells of Bedr, in defiance of the Coreish, and having bartered their goods at leisure, returned to Medina. Mahomet was much pleased at the result of this expedition,—the Second Bedr, as it is called,—and it is noticed with considerable self-gratulation in the Coran. The Coreish were mortified at having left the rendezvous to their enemies, and began to plan a second attack upon Medina. But another year elapsed before the design was carried into effect.

In the summer, tidings came from the north that marauding bands, driven by the famine, were plundering travellers on the way to Syria, and that they even threatened a descent upon Medina. To clear the country of these bandits, Mahomet set out at the head of a thousand men, and marched as far as Dûma and the Syrian confines. The freebooters were dispersed, and a treaty was made with Oyeina, chief of the powerful Fezâra tribe, for the right to graze on certain lands in Nejd, where forage was still procurable. The campaign, though in itself uneventful, was of some importance in spreading the terror of the prophet's name in the north, and also as inuring his followers to the hardship of long marches at the hottest season of the year.

Campaign to Dûma and Syrian frontier, July 626 A.D. A.H. V.

Since his marriage with Haphsa, that is, for above a year, Mahomet had been content with the three inmates of his harem. He now added to the number two other wives. The first was Zeinab, the widow of his cousin Obeida, who fell at Bedr. Noted for her charity, she gained the title of *Mother of the poor;* but she died a year or two after. Within a month of this marriage the prophet took to wife Omm Salma, whose husband had recently died of wounds received at Ohod. Though still beautiful, this lady was no longer young, and at first excused herself from the prophet's suit on the plea of mature age and a rising family. But Mahomet set aside the objection by the remark that he too was advanced in

Marriage with Zeinab and Omm Salma, January and February, 626 A.D.

years, and that her children should be his care. After the marriage he tarried three days with his bride, a precedent followed by Moslem husbands when they bring fresh wives into their households.

Mahomet enamoured of his adopted son's wife, June 626 A.D.

Mahomet was now going on to threescore years; but weakness for the sex seemed only to grow with age, and the attractions of his increasing harem were insufficient to prevent his passion from wandering beyond its ample limits. Happening one day to visit the dwelling of his adopted son Zeid, he found him absent. As he knocked, Zeinab, wife of Zeid, started up in confusion to array herself decently for the prophet's reception. But her charms had already through the half-opened door unveiled themselves too freely before his admiring gaze; and Mahomet, smitten by the sight, exclaimed, "*Gracious Lord! Good Heavens! How thou dost turn the hearts of men!*" The words, uttered as he turned to go, were overheard by Zeinab, and she, proud of her conquest, was nothing loth to tell her husband of it. Zeid went at once to Mahomet, and offered to divorce his wife for him. "Keep thy wife to thyself," he answered, "and fear God." But the words fell from unwilling lips. Zeid was ten years younger than Mahomet, but he was short and ill-favoured; and now that Zeinab seemed to court so distinguished an alliance, he probably did not care to keep her any longer as his wife. And so he formally divorced her. The prophet hesitated. The husband had been publicly adopted by him, and as such was known as "Zeid the son of Mahomet." Even in Arabia, to marry the divorced wife of an adopted son was a thing unheard of, and he foresaw the scandal it would create. But the flame would not be stifled. And so, casting his scruples to the winds, he resolved at last to have her. Sitting by Ayesha, the prophetic ecstasy seemed to come upon him. As he recovered, smiling he said, "Who will run and tell Zeinab that the Lord hath joined her to me in marriage?" The maid Salma made haste to carry the tidings to Zeinab. She was overjoyed, and in token of pleasure bestowed upon the messenger all the jewels she had upon her person. Mahomet made no delay. He celebrated the nuptials by a feast in the court of the Mosque, and thus took a second Zeinab to be his wife.

Marries her.

The marriage caused no small obloquy, and to save his reputation Mahomet fell back upon his oracle. A passage was promulgated which purports on the part of the Almighty to sanction the union, and even reprehends the prophet for hesitating to consummate it, from the fear of man. The curious reason is assigned for this marriage, and for the Divine sanction of the same, that the Arabian notion of consanguinity between an adoptive father and his adoptive son, must thus be disallowed:—

And justifies the marriage by a revelation.

When thou, O prophet, saidst to him on whom the Lord hath bestowed favours, and thou too hast bestowed favours,[1] *Keep thy wife to thyself, and fear God;* thou didst conceal in thy breast that which God was minded to make known, and fearedst man,—whereas God is more worthy to be feared.

Sura xxxiii.

And when Zeid had fulfilled her divorce, We joined thee with her in marriage, that there might hereafter be no offence to believers in marrying the wives of their adopted sons, after that

---

1 Meaning Zeid, whom Mahomet had freed and adopted. In the verse following Zeid is mentioned *by name*, the only instance in which any one of the Companions is mentioned by name in the Coran.

they have divorced them. And the command of the Lord is to be observed. . . .

God hath not given a man two hearts within him; . . . neither hath He made your adopted sons your real sons. . . . This your speech proceedeth from your mouths; but God speaketh the truth and directeth in the right way. Let your adopted sons go by their natural father's names. This is more just with God.

Strange to say, the scandal was removed by this "revelation," and thenceforward Zeid was called not the son of Mahomet, but "Zeid the son of Hârith."

About this time the ordinance of "the Veil" was established for the female sex. The reason for its imposition, we are told, was that the Moslem women were exposed to rude remarks from the baser sort as they walked abroad. But the prophet's own recent experience in the unwitting sight of Zeinab's charms was perhaps a stronger reason. Out of this command, as enjoined in the verse quoted from the Coran below, have grown the stringent usages of the Harem and Zenana, which with more or less of seclusion prevail throughout the Moslem world. However degrading and barbarous these usages may appear, yet, with its loose code of polygamy and divorce, some restraints of the kind seem almost indispensable in Islam, if only for the maintenance of decency and social order.

The Veil.

Speak unto the believing women, that they restrain their eyes and preserve their modesty, and display not their ornaments, excepting that which cannot be hid. And let them cast their veils over their bosoms and not show their ornaments, saving to their husbands, their fathers, their sons, nephews, slaves, and children.

Sura xxiv.

On his own wives, who lived in the midst of a crowded and busy court, and were some of them young and beautiful, he imposed an even

Special restrictions on Mahomet's wives.

harder rule. No one unless bidden was to enter their apartments; they were not to be spoken to but from behind a curtain; and to slake the last embers of jealousy, a Divine interdict was declared against their ever marrying again. Henceforward they were known as "the Mothers of the Faithful." The passage is curious. How has the fine gold become dim!

Ye Believers! enter not the apartments of the Prophet, excepting ye be called to sup with him, without waiting his convenient time. When ye are bidden, then enter, and when ye have eaten, then disperse. And stay not for familiar talk, for that maketh the prophet uneasy. It shameth him to say this unto you, but God is not ashamed of the truth. And when ye ask anything of his Wives, ask it of them from behind a curtain. This will be more pure for your hearts and for their hearts. It is not becoming that ye should give uneasiness to the Apostle of God, neither that ye should marry his Wives after him for ever. Verily that would be an enormity in the sight of God. . . The prophet is nearer unto believers than their own souls, and his Wives are their Mothers. Sura xxxiii.

A goodly row of modest dwellings, one for each of the six Mothers of the Faithful, now formed the eastern side of the Mosque and of its court. The practice of Mahomet had been to divide his attentions equally amongst his wives. He made the uniform circuit of his harem, spending a day and a night with each. Still, Ayesha's apartment was the one most frequented, and that which best deserved the name of home. His partiality for her provoking discontent among the rest, he did not scruple to release himself from equal obligation to them all by a Divine dispensation. *Postpone the turn of any of thy Wives thou choosest* (such was the oracle) *and admit unto thyself her whom thou mayest desire, as*

Mahomet exempted from equal obligation to his wives.

Sura xxxiii.

well as her whom thou choosest of those whom thou hadst put aside. It will be no offence unto thee. This will be easier, that they may be satisfied and not repine, but be all content with that which thou givest unto them. Could the burlesque of inspiration be carried farther? Yet this verse,—as well as the revelation chiding him because he did not marry Zeinab, and the other passages on the prophet's relations with his household,—are all incorporated in the Coran, and to this day are gravely recited in due course, as a part of the word of God, in every Mosque throughout Islam!

CHAPTER XX.

THE BENI MUSTALICK—MISADVENTURE OF AYESHA.

A.D. 626. A.H. V. ÆTAT. 58.

SOME months after the expedition to Dûma, intelligence was received of fresh designs among the tribes in the neighbourhood of Mecca. Mahomet resolved to anticipate them by attacking the Beni Mustalick, who had mustered their forces with a view to aid the Coreish in their long-talked-of attack upon Medina. The prospect of plunder had made such expeditions so popular, that many of the hitherto disaffected citizens, with Abdallah at their head, rallied round the prophet's standard. The force, therefore, though brought together by various motives, was large; but there were only thirty horse, that arm being still scarce at Medina. They encamped at the wells of Moraisi, near the sea-shore, some marches short of Mecca. There Mahomet had a tent of leather pitched for Ayesha and Omm Salma, his companions in the campaign. The Beni Mustalick were taken by surprise, and the entire tribe captured, with their herds and flocks. Two hundred families, two thousand camels, five thousand sheep, and much household goods, formed the prey, which was distributed amongst the army.

Campaign against Beni Mustalick, Dec. 626. A.H. V.

K

Whilst encamped at Moraisi, an altercation sprang up between the men of Medina and the Refugees, one of the latter having struck a Citizen. High words passed on either side, swords were drawn, and the consequences might have been serious, had not the tumult been appeased in time. During the quarrel the disaffected citizens gave free expression to their disloyal feelings. "This," said Abdallah openly, "ye have brought upon yourselves by inviting these strangers to come amongst us. Wait till we get back to Medina, and then the Mightier shall surely expel the Meaner."

Altercation between Citizens and Refugees.

Mahomet was alarmed at the strife and at the violent language of Abdallah. Bad blood breaking out between the Citizens and Refugees was the one thing fatal to his cause he had to dread. In the fatigue of a long march the quarrel would be smothered and forgotten. Therefore, though the hour was unseasonable, and peace outwardly restored, he gave orders for breaking up the camp. All night he kept the army marching, and next day until the sun was high. Then they halted, and, overcome by weariness, forgot the past in sleep. From thence they proceeded to Medina by ordinary stages.

Mahomet orders hasty march.

Before Mahomet, Abdallah protested that he had not made use of the obnoxious words; and although some around the prophet counselled severe measures, Abdallah's excuse was at the moment received with courtesy. "Leave him alone," said Mahomet to the stern and impatient Omar; "for by my life, so long as he remaineth with us we shall make our companionship pleasant for him." When, however, the prophet found himself re-estab-

Abdallah and followers upbraided in Coran.

lished in the affections of the Citizens, he deemed it necessary to administer a public rebuke to the Disaffected. The message conveying it purports, as usual, to come direct from Heaven. It curses the insincere professors of the faith; and by quoting the very speech of which Abdallah was accused, points the rebuke, notwithstanding his disavowal, specially at him:—

When the Hypocrites come before thee, they say, *We confess that thou art the Prophet of the Lord;* and God knoweth that thou art His prophet, and that the Hypocrites are liars. They are thine enemies. God curse them; how they are turned aside unto lies! . . . These be they that say, *Withhold your goods from the followers of the prophet of God, and so they will disperse.* Whereas unto the Lord belongeth the treasure of heaven and earth. But the Hypocrites understand not. They say, *When we return unto the city* (Medina), *verily the Mightier shall expel from thence the Meaner;* whereas might belongeth unto the Lord and to His prophet and the Believers. But the Hypocrites do not comprehend.

Sura lxiii.

Among the captives brought to Medina was Joweiria, a damsel of birth and beauty, and wife of one of the chiefs of the Mustalick tribe. The Citizen to whose lot she fell demanded a great ransom for her. In despair, she ventured into the presence of Mahomet, and pleaded for some remission. A qualm passed over Ayesha as she saw Mahomet listening to the fair suppliant, and she soon perceived that the conqueror and the captive were exchanging places. "Wilt thou hearken, damsel," he said, "to something that may be better than what thou askest of me?" Marvelling at the softness of his speech, she asked what that might be. "Even that I should pay thy ransom and take thee for myself." The maiden was nothing loth. And so, the ransom paid down, Mahomet took

Mahomet marries one of the captives.

her to wife, and built a seventh house for her reception. On this, the people said that as the Beni Mustalick were now their relatives, they would let all the prisoners go free as Joweiria's dower; "and so," Ayesha used to say, "no woman was ever a greater blessing to her people than this Joweiria."

But a trial severer than the advent of a new rival was at that moment hanging over Ayesha. Her virtue was about to be called in question. When the wives of Mahomet accompanied him on his journeys, they travelled each in a litter borne upon a camel, and shrouded carefully from the public gaze. At the hour of marching the litter was brought up and placed close to the door of the lady's tent; at her leisure she would enter and close the curtain, upon which the bearers would approach, and raising the litter fasten it upon the camel's back. On alighting a corresponding procedure was observed. Ayesha's misadventure happened on the last march of the army on their returning from Moraisi. As they entered Medina, and the litter of Ayesha was put down at her door, it was found to be empty. According to her own account, the incident happened thus. At the last halting-place, in the early morning while it was yet dark, the litter was brought as usual and placed at the door of her tent; but she had dropped her necklace outside, and instead of at once entering the vehicle, she went in search of the missing ornament. On returning she found the litter gone. The bearers, imagining her to have entered (for she was slim and light), had lifted and strapped it upon the camel, and then led the animal away. The tents were all struck, and the place was a still desert. Expecting that when the mistake was discovered the

Misadventure of Ayesha.

litter would be brought back, she wrapped her clothes around her and fell asleep. As the day dawned, a Refugee, Safwân by name, chanced to pass that way, and uttered an exclamation of surprise at finding her thus all alone. She made no answer; and no other words (so Ayesha affirmed) passed between them, excepting this, that Safwân, turning his face away so as not even to see, desired her to mount his camel. Then he approached, and led the camel straightway, with Ayesha seated on it, to Medina. Though making every haste, he failed to overtake the main body of the force; and so, led by Safwân, she entered the city in the gaze of all.

Mahomet's estrangement.

The scandal-loving Arabs were not slow in drawing sinister conclusions from the inopportune affair, and spreading them abroad; and these reaching the ears of Mahomet, caused him much uneasiness. An immediate change of manner towards his favourite wife preyed upon her mind. She fell sick, and learning from a friend the rumours affecting her good name, obtained permission to return to her father's house. The estrangement strengthened the grounds of defamation. Ayesha's fall was gloried over by those who bore the prophet no good will, and even among his staunch adherents it became a topic of malevolent conversation. Such were Abdallah, glad of anything to strengthen his waning authority; Hassân the poet; Hamna daughter of Jahsh, who rejoiced in the disgrace of her sister Zeinab's rival, and others.

He chides her calumniators.

When matters had gone on from bad to worse for several weeks, Mahomet resolved to put an end to the scandal. He mounted the pulpit, and sharply upbraided his followers for meddling in matters which, he said, were no concern of theirs, and for traducing Safwân, against whom not even the shadow of evidence had been advanced. Then he went to the house of Abu Bekr, and took counsel with his friends. Most of these declared their disbelief of the slanderous report. Aly was more guarded, and with an unkindly suggestion—which Ayesha never forgot—that her place could easily be supplied, proposed the examination of her maid. But the maid, when called upon, could only give testimony that, if anything, was in her mistress's favour.

Ayesha declared innocent.

Then Mahomet went to the chamber where Ayesha herself was sitting. From the first hearing of the imputation against her virtue, she had abandoned herself to an excess of grief. Her mother assured her that it was nothing but the common lot of a favourite wife to be traduced by jealous rivals, and that the cloud would pass off. But she refused to be comforted, and continued to pine away. Mahomet, accompanied by her father and mother, sat down beside her and said, "Ayesha, thou hearest what men have spoken of thee. Fear God. If indeed thou art guilty, then repent toward God, for He verily accepteth the repentance of His servants." She held her peace, thinking that her parents would rebut the imputation. At last, bursting into a flood of tears, she protested her innocence. "I am helpless," she said; "if I confess, the Lord knoweth I am clear; if I deny, none believeth me. With Joseph's father I can but say, '*Patience becometh me, and the Lord is my Helper.*'"[1] Mahomet did not speak. As they sat in silence he appeared to fall into a trance. They covered

[1] Quoting from Sura xii. 19. She wished to say *Jacob*, but in the confusion of the moment the name escaped her memory.

him over, and placed a pillow beneath his head. In a little while he sat up, and wiping away the heavy drops from his forehead, exclaimed, "Rejoice, O Ayesha! for the Lord hath declared thine innocence." "Embrace thy husband!" cried her mother. But Ayesha could do no more than ejaculate, "Praise be to the Lord!"

Immediately after, Mahomet went forth and recited in the hearing of the people the oracle which forms the Moslem law of adultery to the present day. Harlotry is punished with the lash. For adultery the penalty is death,[1] but the charge must be sustained by the direct evidence of four eye-witnesses; otherwise, the tables are turned upon the accusers, who are to be scourged with fourscore stripes—the punishment of calumny. Then referring to the slanderers of Ayesha, the passage proceeds thus:— **Law of adultery.**

Wherefore, when they heard of it, did not the faithful men and women imagine good in their hearts, and say, *This is a manifest falsehood?* Have they produced four witnesses thereof? Wherefore since they have not produced the witnesses, they are surely liars in the sight of God. **Sura xxiv.**

If it were not for the favour of God upon you, and His mercy in this world and the next, verily for that which ye have spread abroad, a grievous punishment had overtaken you, when ye published it with your tongues, and spake with your mouths that of which ye had no knowledge. And ye counted it a light thing, but with God it is weighty. Why, when ye heard it, did ye not say, *It is not for us to speak of this; gracious Lord! it is a monstrous calumny!* God admonisheth you that ye return not to the like again for ever. If it had not been for the grace of God upon you and His mercy,—verily God is merciful and forgiving.

---

[1] The mode of punishment is *stoning* of both culprits to death, according to the Jewish law. The law, however, is not now in the Coran, the verse prescribing this having, as the common belief is, dropped out. For *slaves* the punishment is stripes and not death.

And so, after indulging in further denunciations, and threats of punishment both in this world and the next, against the publishers of scandal, Mahomet commanded the prescribed punishment to be inflicted on the traducers of Ayesha. Even Hamna, sister to the favourite Zeinab, did not escape. Abdallah alone was excused, which was fortunate for the prophet; for a time of trial was at hand when the alienation of this still powerful Citizen might have proved dangerous to his cause.

Slanderers of Ayesha scourged.

Satisfied with such emphatic vindication of the honour of his favourite wife, Mahomet dropped the grudge, and sought now rather to conciliate her calumniators. Safwân, the hero of the tale, still smarting from the imputations veiled under Hassân's satire, drew his sword upon him. The quarrel was carried before the prophet, who, having rebuked the poet, more than compensated him for the indignity of the lash by the gift of an estate in the vicinity of Medina.

Hassân conciliated.

Ayesha resumed her place, more secure than ever as the queen of the prophet's heart and home. Hassân, changing his muse, sang of her purity, elegance, and wit, and (what she piqued herself the most upon) her slender, graceful figure. The flattering compliment reconciled her to the poet; but she never forgave Aly for his doubting.

Hassân reconciles Ayesha by an ode.

It is curious to mark how the jealous temperament of Mahomet transpires through such passages of the Coran as the following:—

Mahomet cautions his wives against immodesty.

O prophet, say unto thy Wives, *If ye love the world and the fashions thereof, come, and I will make a provision for you, and dismiss you with a fair dismission.* But if ye seek after God and His Apostle and the life to come, verily the Lord

Sura xxxiii.

hath prepared for them that are good amongst you a great reward. Ye Wives of the Prophet! if any amongst you should be guilty of incontinency, her punishment shall be doubled unto her twofold, and that were easy with God. But she that amongst you devoteth herself to God and to His Apostle, and worketh righteousness, We shall give unto her her reward twofold, and We have prepared for her a gracious maintenance.

O ye Wives of the prophet! ye are not as other women. If ye fear the Lord, be not bland in your speech, lest he indulge desire in whose heart is disease. And abide within your houses, and array not yourselves as in the bygone days of ignorance, and observe the stated times of prayer, and obey God and His Apostle, &c.

The law of evidence for adultery.

The direct evidence of four eye-witnesses is still needed to prove the charge of adultery, so that the draconic penalty is almost inoperative. But the law itself is a fair example of the manner in which the code of Islam grew out of the circumstances of the prophet's life,—concrete, rather than framed upon abstract considerations.

CHAPTER XXI.

SIEGE OF MEDINA. SPRING OF 627 A.D.
A.H. V. ÆTAT. 58.

Combined attack by Coreish and Bedouins on Medina.

WHILE Mahomet thus busied himself with the cares and anxieties of his increasing harem, a storm was brewing in the south. The winter again came round, when it had become the wont of the Coreish to arm themselves against Medina. Their preparations now exceeded those of any previous year. Four thousand men were brought into the field, of whom 300 were cavalry, and 1500 mounted on camels. The Bedouins of Nejd railied round them in great numbers. The Fezâra brought 1000 soldiers mounted on camels, and the Soleim 700. The whole force numbered 10,000 men, marching in three separate columns, but all under the leadership of Abu Sofiân.

Medina defended by a trench. Feb. 627 A.D. A.H. V.

Alarm overspread Medina. The defeat at Ohod by numbers much inferior, put a pitched battle out of the question. By the advice of a Mesopotamian slave, familiar with warlike tactics, Mahomet resolved to entrench Medina, a strategic device as yet unknown in Arabia. The outer line of substantial houses formed in itself a solid defence towards the east, but it was necessary to connect this on one hand with the approaching rocks on the north, and on the other to carry it round the open defenceless quarter on the south-east. Mahomet encouraged the labour of the citizens by himself bearing basket-loads of the excavated earth, and joining in their song, as at the building of the Mosque. In six days the trench was dug. Behind it was an earthen dyke, along which they piled heaps of well-sized stones, to be used against the enemy. The outlying inhabitants were all withdrawn, and the women and children for greater security were bidden to stay upon the flat roofs of the houses. These things were barely finished when the invaders were reported to be advancing as before by the hill of Ohod. The army of Medina, 3000 strong, moved out into the open space between the city and the trench. A tent of red leather was pitched for Mahomet upon the ground, in which he was visited by his wives in turn.

Coreish encamp outside the trench.

The Coreish, and the Bedouin hordes, with their multitude of camels and horses, finding the country deserted, swept round the former field of victory, and still advancing unopposed, were brought to a stand by the trench. Closely guarded all along, it formed a barrier which they could not pass. Disconcerted by the stratagem, they were forced to pitch their camp some little way off, where they contented themselves for a time by the distant discharge of archery.

And detach the Beni Coreitza.

Meanwhile Abu Sofiân succeeded in gaining over the Beni Coreitza, the only remaining Jewish tribe, whose fortress lay two or three miles to the south-west. The news alarmed Mahomet and disturbed the city; for the Jews had still a powerful party in their favour, and the defences, moreover, were weakest on that side. Disaffection lurked on every hand, and some began even to talk of deserting to the enemy. To protect the town in the quarter most exposed, as well as to guard it from treachery within, parties had to be detached from the army, already barely strong enough to man the trench, and by them the city was day and night patrolled. A strong guard was also posted over the prophet's tent.

Attack on trench repulsed.

The vigilance of the Moslem pickets kept at bay the confederate host, who proclaimed the trench to be an unworthy subterfuge. "Truly this ditch," they cried in their chagrin, "is the artifice of strangers, a shift to which no Arab has ever yet stooped." But it was, nevertheless, the safety of Medina. The Coreish tried over and again to force it. Discovering a narrow, ill-guarded spot, they made an attack upon it. Spurring their horses, a few cleared the trench, but were driven back and barely effected their escape after a hand-to-hand encounter, in which Aly brought his adversary to the ground. Next day the whole Meccan army was engaged in the attempt to carry the trench. It required unceasing vigilance to frustrate the design. Now the Confederates would mass their force upon this point, now upon that, and again breaking into columns, they would threaten the whole line at once. Khâlid, by the rapid movement of his troop of horse, distracted the defenders. Once and again a gallant dash was made at the city, and the tent of Mahomet himself was at one moment in peril. But the brave front and galling archery of the citizens drove the assailants back. These tactics were kept up all day long, and even into the night. But the trench was never crossed in force, nor did the troops engage near enough for slaughter. The Moslems lost but five men, and the Confederates three.

But the army of Medina was harassed and weary, though the loss of life was small. The people were dismayed at the surging host that hemmed them in on every side. Beyond the trench they saw their possessions ravaged and destroyed, and they began to ask for leave to go and protect them. Mahomet looked weak before the world. Where now was the heavenly promise? It was a day of rebuke when (as we read in the Coran) "the enemy came upon them from above and from beneath, and the sight was confused, and the hearts reached to the throat, and the people imagined of God strange imaginations; for there the faithful were tried and made to tremble violently." The distress had now lasted ten or twelve days, when it occurred to Mahomet that he might buy off the Bedouins from the Coreish. Negotiations were accordingly opened with Oyeina, their chief, who demanded as his price one-half of the date harvest of Medina. Mahomet had already offered one-third, when he thought it best to call in the leading men of the city to advise him. They spurned the terms; "but," said they, "if thou hast received a command from the Lord in this thing, then follow the same." "Nay," answered the prophet, "if I had received a bidding from the Lord, I had not consulted you; I ask you but as to that thing which is the most expedient." "Then," said the chiefs, "give them nought but the sword." And so the matter dropped; but it shows the straits and the apprehensions to which Mahomet was at this time reduced.

Distress at Medina.

Sura xxxiii.

A more artful device was now resorted to. A Bedouin chief, Noeim, was famous for his craft and cunning. He came to Mahomet offering

Dissension sown between Coreitza and Coreish.

his services. They were readily accepted. "See now," said Mahomet to him, "whether thou canst not break up this confederacy; for war after all is a game at deception." So Noeim, going first to the one side and then to the other, sowed the seeds of distrust between them. When, therefore, the allied chiefs summoned the Jews to join them, as they had agreed, in a combined attack upon the city, these pleaded as an excuse the Sabbath day: and moreover, affecting fear of being deserted by the Confederate host, demanded hostages of them. This was nothing more than what Noeim had told the Coreish to be on their guard against, and so it appeared fully to confirm his report of Jewish treachery.

A storm bursts, and Coreish depart.

The Confederate chiefs were already disheartened. Every attempt to carry the trench had failed. Success had been hoped for in a general engagement, during which the Beni Coreitza were to fall on Mahomet's defenceless rear, but instead of this they began to dread an attack from the Coreitza themselves. Supplies ran short, and the camels were dying rapidly. Wearied and damped in spirit, the night set in upon them with drenching rain and tempest. The ground became a swamp; tents were blown down, fires extinguished, and even the cooking-pots and equipage were overthrown. Cold and comfortless, and despairing now of any turn of fortune, Abu Sofiân resolved on an immediate march. Calling the chiefs around him, he cried, "Break up the camp; as for me, I am gone!" With these words he leapt upon his camel and led the way, Khâlid bringing up the rear with his troop of horse. They took the road again by Ohod for Mecca, and the Bedouins retired to their haunts in the desert.

The glad intelligence soon reached Mahomet. As

morning dawned not a man of the great host was left in sight. It was, the prophet said, the result of Divine interposition in answer to the prayers of his people. For some days he is said to have offered up this petition:—"O Lord, Revealer of the Book, Thou that art swift in taking account! turn to flight the Confederate host. Turn them to flight, O Lord, and make them to quake!" The Lord had sent the tempestuous wind, he said. The armies of heaven had been fighting for them; terror had been struck into the heart of the enemy; and now they were gone.

Relief ascribed by Mahomet to Divine interposition.

CHAPTER XXII.

FATE OF THE BENI COREITZA. 627 A.D. A.H. V.

Beni Coreitza besieged, March 627 A.D. A.H. V.

THE army of Medina now joyfully broke up their camp, in which they had been besieged fifteen days, and returned to their homes. Mahomet had no thought of hanging on the enemy's rear, as he had done before, or of exposing his force to an action in the open country. A still more important blow might be struck, and that without danger, nearer home. He was still cleansing himself from the dust of the field, when suddenly the order went forth for the army to reform and march against the Jews. Gabriel, he said, had descended and reproached him with laying aside his armour while as yet the Angels had not laid theirs aside. "Arise!" cried the heavenly visitant,—"arise, go up against the stronghold of the Coreitza. Behold, I go before you to shake the foundations thereof." The great banner, yet unfurled, was placed in the hands of Aly, and the prophet, mounting his ass, led the way. By the time of evening prayer the Moslem army, as before three thousand strong, was encamped beneath the walls of the fortress. They had, however, to retire a little distance, for, approaching too near, one had been killed by a mill-stone cast by a Jewess from the walls. The place was then closely invested, and entirely cut off from the outer world. The imprudent Jews, whom their brethren's fate should have taught to better purpose than to dally with the Confederate army, were soon reduced to great distress. They offered to capitulate on condition of exile, even empty-handed. But Mahomet, bent on a sterner revenge, refused to listen.

They surrender.

At length the wretched garrison, brought to the verge of starvation, offered to surrender on condition that their fate were left to the judgment of their old allies, the Beni Aus. To this Mahomet agreed; and so, when the siege had now lasted several weeks, the tribe, numbering over two thousand souls, came down from their stronghold. The men, with hands pinioned behind their backs, were kept apart. The women and children, torn from their protectors, were placed under charge of a renegade Jew; but one, the beautiful Rihâna, was kept by Mahomet for himself. The spoil, consisting of household stuff, armour, flocks, and herds, was put aside to await the arbitrament of the Beni Aus. All store of wine and fermented liquor was poured forth, as now forbidden to believers.

Sád appointed arbiter.

The Beni Aus, with whom the judgment lay, were urgent with the prophet that their ancient allies should be spared. "They are *our* confederates," they cried importunately. "Show them at least the same pity as, at the suit of the Beni Khazraj, was shown to *their* confederates, the Beni Nadhîr." "Are ye content then," said Mahomet, "that they be judged by one of yourselves?" They answered Yes; and Mahomet nominated Sád, a chief of their tribe, to be the arbiter. This man had been struck by an arrow at the trench, and friendship for his old allies had been turned by their treachery into bitter hate. Though convalescent, he was still nursed in a tent which had been pitched for the wounded in the court of the Mosque. Large and corpulent, he was now mounted with difficulty upon an ass, and, amidst appeals for mercy from his tribesmen who crowded round him, conducted to the camp. On the way he answered not a word, till, drawing near the spot, he said, "Verily to Sád this grace hath been given, that in the cause of God he careth not for any blame the blamers may cast upon him." Assisted to alight, he was called on to deliver judgment. The people still were urging mercy. He turned to them. "Will ye then," said he, "bind yourselves by the covenant of the Lord, that whatsoever be my judgment, ye shall accept the same?" There was a murmur of assent. "Then," proceeded Sád, "my judgment is, that the men shall be put to death, the women and children sold into slavery, and the spoil divided amongst the army." A thrill of horror must have run through the assembled host; but all questioning was stopped by Mahomet, who sternly ratified the verdict. "Truly," said he, "the judgment of Sád is the judgment of the Lord, pronounced on high from above the Seventh heaven."

His bloody judgment.

The camp broke up, and the people wended their way to the city. The prisoners followed. The men were shut up in a yard separate from the women and children, and spent the hours of darkness in repeating passages from their Scriptures, and exhorting one another to faith and constancy. During the night trenches were dug across the market-place. In the morning Mahomet, himself a spectator, commanded the male captives to be brought out in companies of five

Butchery of the tribe.

and six at a time. As each party came up they were made to sit down in a row on the brink of the trench, beheaded, and their bodies cast therein. And so with company after company until all were slain. One woman only was put to death,—it was she who threw the mill-stone from the battlements. When told that her husband had been executed, she loudly avowed what she had done, and demanded of Mahomet that she might share her husband's fate,—a petition which, perhaps in more mercy than was meant, he granted. This heroine's smile, as she stepped fearless and cheerful to her death, Ayesha tells us haunted her ever after. Quarter was obtained by friends for Zoheir and his household. "But what," inquired this aged man, "of all our other chiefs,—of Kab, and Howey, and Ozzâl the son of Samuel?" As he named one and another there came the same reply—they had all been slain. "Then," cried he, "of what use any longer is life to me? Leave me not in the tyrant's power who hath beheaded all the rest. I will go with them to my home. Here, take this sword; it is sharp. Strike hard and high." When told of his dying words, Mahomet answered, "Yea, he shall join them in their home,—the fire of hell."

Mahomet takes Rihâna as concubine.

The butchery lasted all day, and continued by torchlight into the evening. Having thus drenched the market-place with the blood of seven or eight hundred Jewish victims, and commanded the ground to be smoothed over their remains, Mahomet retired to solace himself with Rihâna. The husband and male relatives of this poor lady had all perished in the massacre. He offered her marriage, but she preferred to remain his bond-maid. She declined Islam, but she had no escape from the embrace of her licentious conqueror. She did not many years survive her unhappy fate.

Women and booty distributed.

There were a thousand captive women, besides the little ones who counted with their mothers. From his own share Mahomet made gifts to certain of his friends of some of the fairer of the maidens thus reduced to slavery. The rest of the women and children he sent to Nejd, to be sold in exchange for horses and arms in the service of the state. The rest of the captives and the booty—cattle, lands, and chattels—were sold as prize, or taken over as their share by the three thousand men who had invested the fortress.

Death and burial of Sád.

We may now follow Sád to his end. Having delivered his bloody decree, he was again seated on his ass, and conducted back to the hospital tent at the Mosque. But the excitement had been too great. The wound broke out afresh, and he sank. Mahomet hastened to the bedside, and placing Sád's head upon his knee, prayed over him: "O Lord; truly Sád hath laboured in Thy service, and hath fulfilled his covenant. Wherefore do Thou receive his spirit, with the best reception of a departing soul." The dying man whispered his parting salutation in the prophet's ear and expired. As they carried him out to burial, his mother made loud lamentation over him in elegiac verse. "Leave her alone," said Mahomet, as they chided her to hold her peace; "leave her thus alone; all other poets lie but she." Notwithstanding the corpulence of the deceased, the bier appeared marvellously light, and some superstitiously attributed it to the bloody judgment. Mahomet with ready response turned aside the malignant omen, telling the people, "The angels bear the bier, and therefore it is light. The throne on high vibrateth for Sád; the portals of heaven are thrown open, and seventy thousand angels are following him that never trod the earth before." As they lowered the body Mahomet shuddered and changed colour, but recovering himself, gave thanks and raised the *takbîr*, "Great is the Lord," which, taken up by the great assembly, resounded far and near. His change of colour he explained thus: "At that moment the grave became strait for Sád, and the sides thereof closed in upon him. Verily, if any one could have escaped the straitening of the grave it had been Sád. Then the Lord gave him freedom therein." He comforted his mother, who stood by, and when they would have held her back, suffered her to have a last look at her son's remains. He lingered while they levelled the spot, and sprinkled it over with water. Then praying once more for the departed chief, he turned and went to his home.

Blot left by massacre of B. Coreitza.

The massacre of the Beni Coreitza was a barbarous deed which cannot be justified by any reason of political necessity. There was, no doubt, a sufficient cause for attacking them, and even for severely punishing the leaders who had joined the enemy at so critical a moment. Mahomet might also have been justified in making them quit altogether a neighbourhood in which they formed a dangerous nucleus of disaffection at home, and an encouragement for attack from abroad. But the indiscriminate slaughter of the whole tribe cannot but be recognized as an act of enormous cruelty, which casts an odious blot upon the prophet's name.

Certain renegades.

Three or four men of the doomed tribe purchased their lives, their families, and their property at the expense of their ancestral creed.

So also, no doubt, might others, and, indeed, the whole tribe, have bought their safety. But they remained staunch to Judaism, and in the strictest sense may be accounted martyrs to their faith.

Political effect of the massacre.

The sanguinary fate of the Coreitza removed the last remnant of open opposition, political or religious, from the neighbourhood of Medina. It did not, indeed, at the moment, escape hostile criticism; but it struck terror into the heart of every disloyal citizen. And the prophet was invested with a halo so supernatural, and to his enemies so dreadful, that no one dared outwardly to signify dissent. The successful defence of the city also in the recent siege, conducted on the responsibility of Mahomet as its now recognized ruler, had greatly strengthened his prestige. The whole weight of the Coreish and of the tribes of Nejd had been repulsed, and that with hardly any loss. These incidents are dwelt upon at considerable length in the Coran. The following are some extracts:—

Sura xxxiii.

O ye that believe! call to mind the favour of the Lord unto you, when a multitude came up against you, and We sent upon them a tempest, and Hosts which ye saw not.

When the Hypocrites and those diseased in heart said, *God and His prophet have promised you only a delusion;* and a party said, *O men of Yathreb! there is here no security for you, wherefore retire;* and others asked leave of the prophet to depart, saying, *Our homes are unprotected;* and they were not unprotected, but they desired only to escape. . . SAY, Flight will not profit you, if you were to flee from death and slaughter; and even if it did, ye would enjoy this life but for a little space.

When fear cometh, thou mayest, O Prophet, see them looking towards thee, their eyes rolling, like unto one that is overshadowed with death. Then when the fear hath gone, they attack thee with sharp tongues, covetous of the choicest of the spoil. They thought that the Confederates[1] would not depart. And if the

[1] That is, the Coreish and their Bedouin allies.

Confederates should come again, they would wish themselves away amongst the Bedouins, asking tidings of you. And if they were amongst you, they would not fight excepting but a little. . . The Lord drove back the Heathen in their rage; they obtained no advantage. And God sufficeth for the Believers in battle. He is strong and mighty.

And He hath caused to descend from their strongholds the Jews that assisted them. And He struck terror into their hearts. A part ye slaughtered, and a part ye took into captivity. And He hath made you to inherit their lands, their habitations, and their wealth.

CHAPTER XXIII.

SIXTH YEAR OF THE HEGIRA. A.D. 627, 628.
A.H. VI. ÆTAT. 59.

Numerous minor expeditions. A.H. VI.

MEDINA now entered on a year of comparative repose, the Sixth of the Hegira. No campaign of any importance was undertaken. Small armed bands were, however, frequently in motion for the chastisement of hostile tribes, the repulse of bandits, and the pursuit of caravans. There were during the year as many as seventeen such expeditions, one of which reached as far as to Dûma. These generally ended in the capture of herds and flocks or other booty, and served to spread the terror of the prophet's name.

Capture of Abul Aas, Mahomet's son-in-law.

On one occasion an interesting episode occurred. A well-freighted caravan from Mecca, venturing to resume the sea-shore route to Syria, was overpowered and carried into Medina. Among the prisoners was Abul Aas, husband of Zeinab, the prophet's daughter. While declining to embrace the faith of Mahomet, this man had equally resisted the bidding of the Coreish to divorce his daughter. The attachment was mutual, for when the emigration to Medina took place, Zeinab chose to stay behind at Mecca with her husband. He fought at Bedr, and was taken prisoner to Medina. For his ransom Zeinab sent her jewels. One was a necklace which Khadîja had given her on her marriage.

Mahomet was touched by the affecting memorial, and said to the people, "If it seem right in your eyes, let my daughter's husband go free, and send these trinkets back." So Abul Aas was set free, on condition that he would send Zeinab to her father. He kept his promise. But as she was leaving Mecca, Zeinab was pursued by some of the baser sort, and by them so roughly handled as to bring on a miscarriage. It was three or four years after this incident that Abul Aas now again fell into the hands of the Moslems. As the party carrying him captive approached Medina, he contrived by night to have an interview with Zeinab, who gave him the guarantee of her protection. At morning prayer she called aloud from her apartment, which adjoined the court of the Mosque, that she had passed her word to Abul Aas. When prayers were ended, Mahomet said to the assembly, "Ye have heard, as I have, the words of my daughter. I protest to you that I knew nothing of it till this moment. But the pledge of even the least of my followers must needs be kept." Thereupon the captors resigned their claim, and Abul Aas was suffered to go free. He returned to Mecca; but the attachment of his wife so wrought upon him, that having there settled his affairs, he made profession of Islam, and rejoined her at Medina. The following year she died of disease resulting from the attack made upon her at Mecca. Her treatment on that occasion had so incensed the prophet, that on hearing of it he threatened, if the perpetrators fell into his hands, to have them burned alive. But on second thought he countermanded the order, and said, "It is not fitting that any of His creatures should punish by fire, but God only. Wherefore, if ye seize them, put them simply to the sword."

A small expedition to the north may be mentioned for the cruel deed which closed it. A caravan from Medina was waylaid by a marauding tribe on the road to Syria, the freight plundered, and the convoy maltreated. The citizens were exasperated at the loss, and a strong party set out to punish the offenders. They surprised and captured the bandits' stronghold. Omm Kirfa, who had gained celebrity as the mistress of this den of robbers, was taken prisoner with her daughter. Neither the sex nor the advanced age of this lady saved her from a death of great barbarity. Her limbs were bound each to a separate camel, and these driven different ways, she was thus torn in pieces. Others of the family were also put to death. Zeid, who led the expedition, hastened to tell his success to Mahomet, who embraced and kissed him. We hear of no disapprobation at the inhuman treatment of the aged female. The daughter was given to Ayesha as her waiting-maid; but the brigand spirit survived in her, and a few years after we find her slain in a similar encounter with the troops of Khâlid.[1]

Barbarous execution of a Bedouin lady.

Another cruel punishment led to a special provision in the code of Islam. A party of eight Bedouins visited Medina and embraced the faith. But the damp affected their spleen, and as a remedy, Mahomet bade them join a herd of camels grazing in the vicinity, and drink their milk. With returning health there revived also the lust of plunder. They escaped with the herd, and when pursued, slew the herdsman, cut off his limbs, and mangled his body. Twenty horsemen sent in pursuit seized the culprits and brought them back to Medina. Justly incensed

And of certain Bedouin robbers.

[1] See *Annals of the Early Caliphate*, p. 27.

at their savage crime, Mahomet was betrayed into an act of greater inhumanity. The arms and legs of the eight men were cut off, and their eyes put out. The sightless, shapeless trunks were then impaled upon the plain till life was extinct. On reflection, the prophet felt that he had exceeded the bounds of humanity, and a passage was revealed which limited the punishment for such offence to cutting off the hands, and in some cases also the feet, of the robber, male or female; and this is the barbarous law of Islam to the present day.

With the extinction of the Jews there comes a change over the subject matter of the Coran. Invective against the ancient people of God, and the lengthy tales borrowed from their Scripture and legends, with which the oracle had hitherto teemed, now entirely disappear. Tame in its diction, the "Revelation" becomes more and more confined as a rule to the promulgation of orders based on the incidents of the day. Some of these are curious. For example, on one occasion at prayers the Mosque was suddenly emptied at the sound of drums announcing the return of a caravan, and the prophet was left standing in the pulpit alone. The breach of decorum is thus noticed in a passage purporting, like the rest of the Coran, to be a message from heaven:—

Revelations of the period.

> O Believers! when ye hear the call to prayer on the day of assembly (Friday), then hasten to the commemoration of God, and leave off trafficking. That will be better for you, if ye knew it.
>
> And when the Prayers are ended, then disperse over the land as ye list, and seek gain from the Lord; and make frequent mention of God, that ye may prosper. But when they see merchandise or sport, at once they break away, flocking thereto, and leave thee

Sura lxii.

standing in the pulpit by thyself. SAY, That which is with the Lord is better than sport or merchandise. And God is the best supporter.

Wine, games of chance, and usury forbidden.

In another passage the prophet chides his followers for coming to the services of the Mosque in a state of inebriety. At the first the use of wine, although discouraged, was not absolutely forbidden. But eventually it was proscribed, in company with games of chance and other "works of Satan":—

Sura v.

O believers! verily wine, and the casting of lots, and images and divining arrows, are an abomination of the works of Satan. Shun them, therefore, that ye may prosper. Satan seeketh to sow dissension and hatred among you by means of wine and lots, and to divert you thereby from the remembrance of God, and from prayer. Will ye not therefore abstain?

Such is still the ordinance of Islam.[1] Usury also, in accordance with the Jewish code, is strictly forbidden.

Description of the Deity.

In the midst of the strange medley of laws and regulations, and matters military, religious, and social, forming the staple of the "revelations" of this period, we come ever and anon on passages of lofty flight and eloquence, especially those on the Deity, His Works, and Providence. Such is the following:—

Sura ii. 256.

GOD! There is no God but He, the Living, the Eternal. Slumber doth not overtake Him, neither sleep. To Him belongeth whatsoever is in heaven and earth. Who is he that shall intercede before Him, excepting only by His permission? He knoweth what is before them, and what is behind (*i.e.* the future and the past); and they shall not comprehend anything of His knowledge,—saving in so far as He pleaseth. His throne stretches both over the heavens and over the earth, and the maintenance of both is no burden to Him. He is the lofty and the great.

---

[1] Wherever strict Mahometan rule prevails, indulgence in wine is punished with the lash.

CHAPTER XXIV.

THE UNFULFILLED PILGRIMAGE—TREATY OF HODEIBIA. MARCH 628 A.D. END OF A.H. VI. ÆTAT. 59.

Desire to revisit Káaba.

SIX years had passed since Mahomet and his Companions had seen their native city or worshipped at its shrine, and they pined to revisit it again. Mahomet himself had not ceased to enjoin the pilgrimage of Mecca as an essential part of the new religion. He upbraided the Coreish with hindering the approach of faithful pilgrims, while they desecrated by idolatrous rites the purity of the ancient worship:—

Sura viii.

> Wherefore should not the Lord chastise them? for that they have hindered His servants from visiting the sacred Temple. And they are not the Guardians thereof; verily, none are its Guardians save the pious. But their prayers at the Temple are nought but whistling through their fingers, and the clapping of their hands. So shall ye taste the chastisement of your infidelity.

Mahomet's dream of pilgrimage.

But precept should be enforced by example, and so Mahomet felt that an effort must be made to carry out in company with his followers this the grand rite of Islam. Musing thus, the prophet had by night a vision, in which as in a dream he seemed to see himself and his people enter Mecca peacefully worshipping at the Káaba. He divulged the dream to his followers, who, equally with himself, all yearned for its fulfilment. It was the holy month of Żulcada, preceding the annual pilgrimage,—a month in which, by the sense of Arabia, war was forbidden as a sacrilege, and in which, moreover, observance of the Lesser Pilgrimage was specially meritorious.[1] The resolution accordingly was formed of proceeding on this pilgrimage at once. There was now the chance of a peaceful entry, and if the Coreish should hinder them, the blame would be upon their head.

Mahomet sets out on Lesser Pilgrimage, Feb. 628. A.H. VI.

That the cavalcade should be the more imposing, Mahomet summoned the friendly Bedouin tribes around to join the pilgrimage. But there being no inducement on the score of plunder, most of these, pleading engagement at home, held back. The people of Medina, however, Citizens as well as Refugees, responded eagerly to the call, and forthwith prepared for pilgrimage by putting on the two shreds of clothing which form the sole dress of the devotee. At the first halting-place the prophet and his followers consecrated themselves to the service by uttering the cry, *Labbeik, Labbeik!* "Here am I, O Lord; here am I!" The victims were then set apart by ornaments hung round their necks and by marks upon their sides. Seventy camels were thus devoted to sacrifice, and among them that of Abu Jahl, taken at Bedr. The pilgrim band, numbering fifteen hundred, then moved forward. They presented a peaceful array, carrying only the customary arms of a traveller,—sheathed sword with bow and well-filled quiver. A troop of horse,

[1] For the Lesser Pilgrimage, which is short and simple in its rules, see chap. iii. p. 26.

however, marched in front to give notice of danger. Mahomet carried Omm Salma with him.

The approach of Mahomet, his pious purpose and unwarlike attitude notwithstanding, filled the Coreish with apprehension. Soon under arms, they occupied the Medina road, resolved to bar his entry to the last extremity. A body of two hundred horse, under Khâlid and Ikrima son of Abu Jahl, marched in front. The pilgrims were still two stages from Mecca, when a scout returned to Mahomet with this intelligence:—"The Coreish occupy the road in force; fierce, and clothed as it were in panther skins, their wives and children with them, they swear that they will rather die than let thee pass." The Meccan cavalry now came in sight, and further advance without a battle being impossible, Mahomet turned to the right, and by devious and fatiguing pathways reached Hodeibia, an open space on the immediate verge of the sacred territory surrounding Mecca. There his camel, planting her fore-legs firmly on the ground, refused to stir another step. "She is weary," said the people, as they urged her on. "Nay," cried Mahomet, "Al Caswa is not weary; but the same band restraineth her as aforetime held back the elephant.[1] By the Lord! no petition to respect the sanctity of the Holy city shall be unheard by me this day." A spring of water was found, and they encamped upon the spot.

Coreish oppose entry into Mecca.

The Coreish now sent messengers to ascertain the intentions of Mahomet. Deputations several times went to and fro. At last Othmân, being a chief of family and influence, was sent into the

Deputation of Othmân to Mecca.

[1] Alluding to the deliverance of Mecca, just before the birth of Mahomet, when the Ethiopians from Yemen invaded Mecca with an army followed by an elephant.

city by the prophet to treat with the Coreish. On hearing what he had to say, they made this answer, that if Othmân chose he might himself repair to the Káaba and worship there; but as for Mahomet, they had sworn that this year he should not enter within the precincts of the city. Othmân retired bearing the message. Meanwhile there had been great excitement in the pilgrim camp. As Othmân's return was long delayed, the rumour spread of treachery. The people ran together, and Mahomet, taking his stand beneath the shade of an acacia tree, required of them a solemn pledge to the death, that they would recover their detained comrade. When all had taken the oath, striking each one the palm of his hand on that of the prophet, he himself struck his own right hand upon his left, in token that he would stand by his absent son-in-law. Their fears were soon relieved by the return of Othmân; but "the Pledge of the Tree" is one of those romantic scenes of devotion that are never forgotten, and stand out as landmarks in the early annals of Islam.

The Pledge of the Tree.

In the end a deputation of the Coreish visited Hodeiba with power to conclude terms of peace. Mahomet called for Aly to write them down at his dictation;—

Treaty with the Coreish.

"*In the name of God, most Merciful and Gracious,*" the prophet began. "Stop," cried the others; "as for God, we know Him, but this new name we know it not." "Then write," rejoined Mahomet calmly, "*In thy name, O God! The conditions of peace between Mahomet the prophet of the Lord, and—*" "Stop again," interposed the Meccan chiefs. "If thou wert what thou sayest, we had not armed against thee. Write, as the custom is, but thine own name and thy father's." Still unmoved, Mahomet continued: "*Write then,—between Mahomet son of Abdallah, and Soheil son of Amr.*" The terms were shortly these. War to be suspended for ten years, and amity restored. Chiefs and tribes to be at liberty to join, at their discretion, either side. Converts at Mecca (with reservation of the rights of guardians) should be free to depart for Medina. Mahomet and his followers to retire at once without entering the city; but with permission the following year to return unarmed, and spend three days in pilgrimage at Mecca. Such was the treaty now duly witnessed by the leading men on either side.

Return from Hodeibia.

There being thus left no present prospect of worshipping at the Káaba, Mahomet and his followers contented themselves with fulfilling such of the pilgrim vows as the place admitted of. They sacrificed the victims, and then shaved their heads. And so, after a stay of ten or fifteen days, they quitted Hodeibia on their homeward march. The people were downcast at the abortive issue of the pilgrimage. But the oracle was at hand to raise their drooping spirits. As they journeyed the word passed round that "inspiration had descended on the prophet." From all sides they hastened towards him. Then in the midst of a great assembly, Mahomet, standing upright upon his camel, recited a Sura entitled "The Victory." It opens thus:—

Passages of Coran regarding this expedition.

Sura xlviii.

Verily We have given thee an evident Victory: that God may pardon thee the sin which is past, . . and fulfil His favours upon thee; and that God may assist thee with a glorious assistance.

It then proceeds with a scathing denunciation of

the Arabs of the desert, who by false pretences had excused themselves from joining in the pilgrim journey. Their brave words would be put to the trial in battle "with a people terrible in war;" and meanwhile, as the penalty of malingering—a penalty hateful to the Bedouin—they were forbidden to join in any warlike expedition or to share in its plunder. The Faithful are next applauded for their constancy at "the Pledge of the Tree." It was the hand of God, not the mere hand of the prophet, which then they struck:—

> Verily the Lord was well pleased with the Believers when they pledged themselves to thee under the Tree. He knew what was in their hearts, and He caused tranquillity to descend upon them, and granted them a speedy Victory, and spoils which they shall hereafter take. God hath promised you great spoil, and He hath sent you this Truce beforehand. He restrained the hands of men from you. . . If the Unbelievers (*i.e.* the Coreish) had fought against you, verily they had turned their backs. . . It is the Lord that restrained their hands from you, and your hands from them in the Vale of Mecca. (Then, after denouncing the Coreish)—Now hath the Lord verified unto His Apostle the vision in truth. Ye shall surely enter the Holy temple, if it please God, in security, your heads shaven and your hair shorn. And He hath appointed you after that a speedy Victory besides.

Sura xlviii.

Advantages gained by treaty.

When the recitation was ended, a bystander exclaimed, "An evident victory! where is it?" "Yea," answered Mahomet, "by Him in whose hand is my breath, it is a Victory." Another reminded him of the promise that they should enter Mecca and worship at the Káaba unmolested. "True," he replied; "the Lord indeed hath promised this; but when did He promise it for this year?" In truth Mahomet had gained a real victory. He had forced the Coreish to recognize him as a power to be treated with on equal terms; and liberty had been accorded every one to join Islam at his discretion. "In the two years that followed," writes one of his biographers, "as many persons entered the faith as there belonged to it altogether before, or even more." "And the proof of this," adds another, "is that whereas Mahomet went forth to Hodeibia with only fifteen hundred followers to the pilgrimage, he was followed two years later, in the attack on Mecca, by ten thousand."

CHAPTER XXV.

EMBASSIES DESPATCHED IN VARIOUS DIRECTIONS.
A.D. 628. A.H. VII. ÆTAT. 60.

Despatches to surrounding Potentates, A.D. 628. A.H. VII.

About this time Mahomet formed the singular design of sending despatches to the various Potentates around, acquainting them with the Mission he had received from heaven, denouncing idolatry, and proclaiming the Unity of God. It was suggested to him that the kings of the earth accepted no communication of the kind unless attested with a seal. Therefore he had one of silver engraved with the words, *Mahomet Apostle of God.* Seven letters were accordingly written, and sealed with the seal. Six couriers, each the bearer of such a despatch, were sent forth at the opening of the Seventh year of the Hegira to the courts of Greece and Persia, and some other countries round about.

Letter to the Emperor Heraclius.

Heraclius had recently achieved a splendid success over the arms of Persia, and was at this time engaged in a pilgrimage to Jerusalem on foot, in thankful celebration of his victories, and the recovery of "the true Cross." Just then the letter of Mahomet was forwarded to him by the governor of Bostra, into whose hands it had been delivered by an

Arab messenger. The despatch was addressed to the Emperor himself, and in strange accents, like the voice of a prophet of old, summoned him to recognize the mission of the new apostle, abandon the idolatrous worship of Jesus and his Mother, and return to the Catholic faith of the Unity. It was probably cast aside, or preserved haply as the curious effusion of some harmless fanatic. A similar despatch addressed to Hârith,[1] prince of the Beni Ghassân (Christian Arabs of the Syrian desert), was by him forwarded to the court of Heraclius, with the request that he might be allowed to chastise the audacious impostor. But the Emperor, regarding this cry from the desert as beneath his notice, forbade the expedition, and bid Hârith join him and swell his train as he approached Jerusalem. The King of Persia treated the letter sent to him with still less respect; for, on hearing its contents, we are told that he tore it scornfully in pieces. "Even thus, O Lord," said Mahomet, when told of it, "wilt Thou rend the Tyrant's kingdom from him." Little wot the Kaiser and the Chosroes that in a few short years their empires would shiver at the very name of the obscure Arabian.

The prince of Beni Ghassân,

And King of Persia.

The envoy to Egypt was courteously entreated by the Governor, and dismissed with a gentle and evasive answer. "I know," he wrote, "that a prophet is to arise; but I believe that it will be in Syria, and not in Arabia. I send for thine acceptance two sisters, bondmaids, such as the Copts affect, also a present of raiment, and a mule for thee to ride upon." The gifts were well suited to the

Governor of Egypt sends reply and two slave girls.

[1] A vassal of the Romans, one of a similar dynasty and name to "*Aretas* the king" noticed by the Apostle, 2 Cor. xi. 32.

prophet's taste. Mary, the fairest of the damsels, was chosen for himself, and her sister presented to Hassân the poet. The mule was white, a rarity admired in Arabia, and was kept by Mahomet to be ridden by himself.

Letters were also sent to Yemen and Yemâma, in the south and centre of the peninsula. The former was at this time governed by a Persian Viceroy, who, being virtually independent, was ready to recognize the claims of Mahomet and the fortunes of the rising faith. The chief of Yemâma made answer: "How beautiful is this revelation to which thou invitest me! I too am a poet and an orator, esteemed by the Arabs. Give me a share in the rule, and I will follow thee." "Had he asked of me," said Mahomet, in disdain, "but an unripe date as his share in the land, I should have refused. Let him perish and his vain-glory with him!" Thus cursed, the chief (we are told) died shortly after.

Yemen and Yemâma.

The court of Abyssinia stood upon a different footing from the rest. Many of the Moslems who took refuge in that land had already found their way back to Arabia, but there still remained fifty or sixty to enjoy the hospitality of the Negus. To the despatch of Mahomet the Prince now replied, embracing the faith of Islam, and expressing regret at his inability to join in person the standard of the prophet. In a separate epistle Mahomet begged of the King, as his representative in the matter, to conclude a betrothal for him with Omm Habîba, the widowed daughter of Abu Sofiân. This lady was a refugee in Abyssinia, where her husband, a convert to Christianity, had died. Though

Abyssinia.

Omm Habîba betrothed by the Negus to Mahomet.

thirty-five years of age, her beauty in earlier days still held a place in the memory of the prophet. By this alliance he not only gratified his passion for the sex (a whole year had passed since his last marriage), but no doubt also hoped to make Abu Sofiân more favourable to his cause. The Negus gallantly performed the part assigned to him in the matrimonial project, and also provided two ships, in which he sent back the remaining exiles. These reached Medina in safety in the seventh year of the Hegira.

The Abyssinian exiles reach Medina, A.D. 628.

CHAPTER XXVI.

CONQUEST OF KHEIBAR. AUTUMN OF 628 A.D. A.H. VII. ÆTAT. 60.

Expedition against Kheibar, Aug. 628 A.D. A.H. VII.

On his way back from Hodeibia, in the spring of the year, Mahomet, as we have seen, had foretold "a speedy victory and spoils in abundance elsewhere."[1] The summer passed quietly, and it was autumn before measures were taken to fulfil the promise. The destined prey was Kheibar, a fertile vale about a hundred miles on the way to Syria. It was a Jewish settlement, and, but for his hatred of the stiff-necked race, the attack was entirely unprovoked. The Moslem army was called suddenly to march. Its numbers were about the same as in the expedition to Hodeibia, sixteen hundred, but greatly stronger in cavalry. The Moslem troop had never before exceeded thirty; it was now two hundred strong. The Bedouin allies would gladly have joined the tempting expedition, but, because they had held back from the Hodeibia pilgrimage, they were not allowed. Omm Salma was again the favoured companion of the prophet.

[1] Sura xlviii., *vide supra*, p. 178.

The vale of Kheibar was studded with fortresses perched upon the rocky eminences rising up amongst the date-groves and luxuriant fields of corn. So rapid was the march and so complete the surprise, that the peasants, issuing in the morning to their work, were startled by confronting a great army, and fled back in dismay within their gates. One by one, before defence was possible, the forts were carried. "*Kharrabat Kheibar*," cried Mahomet, with a jubilant play upon the name, as he passed triumphantly from one stronghold to another; "Kheibar is undone. *Allah Akbar!* great is the Lord! Truly, when I light upon the coasts of any people, woe be unto them in that day!" At last the Jews, having had time and heart to rally round their chief Kinâna, took their stand before the strongest citadel. A severe engagement ensued, in which Aly as usual distinguished himself by signal bravery. Having lost his shield, he seized the lintel of a door, which, Samson-like, he wielded in its stead. There was no resisting the impetuosity of the Moslem charge. The victory was complete. Nearly a hundred men fell on the enemy's side; in the whole campaign the army of Medina lost but nineteen.

The Jews vanquished and Kheibar occupied.

After this defeat the citadel surrendered, on condition that the people should be free to quit the country on giving up all their wealth to the conquerors. In carrying out these terms, the chief Kinâna was accused of dishonestly keeping back part of his treasure, notably the marriage portion of the maiden to whom he had just been married, and whose father had perished in the massacre of the Coreitza. "Where are those vessels of gold," asked Mahomet of the vanquished chief,—"the vessels ye used to lend for their

Kinâna tortured and put to death.

feasts to the men of Mecca?" Kinâna protested that he no longer had them. A recreant Jew divulged the secret place where some valuables lay hid. In the hope of discovering the remainder, "fire was applied to the breast of the Chief till his breath had well-nigh gone;" and at last the wretched captive escaped his misery by death.

His wife taken by Mahomet.

On this, Bilâl was sent to fetch Kinâna's bride, the damsel Safia, just fifteen years of age. Finding her with her cousin, the heartless negro carried both the ladies across the battle-field strewn with the dead, and close by the headless corpse of Kinâna. At the ghastly sight the cousin wildly screamed. "Take the she-devil hence," said Mahomet; but aside he chided Bilâl for his thoughtlessness. "Truly," said the negro, "I did it of purpose, to see their fright." But Mahomet was moved by tenderer feelings. Turning to Safia, he cast his mantle over her, in token that he reserved her for himself. One of his followers had coveted this lady, whose beauty appears to have been well known at Medina, but Mahomet made him content by giving him her cousin.

Mahomet's marriage with Safia.

Safia was nothing loth to transfer her affections to the conqueror, nor did he delay the nuptials. The wedding was celebrated with an abundant feast of dates, butter, and curdled milk. Meanwhile the bride was bathed and suitably arrayed by Omm Salma's maid, and then brought forth to be mounted on the prophet's camel. The people said, "Now we shall see whether he hath taken her for his wife, or as a captive concubine." So when he called for a screen to veil her from the public gaze, they knew that she was taken as his wife. Mahomet lowered his knee to help her up, and she, after some coy demur, placing her foot thereon, climbed up into the litter. Mahomet then taking his seat in front, guided thus the camel in the evening to the bridal tent.

Mahomet partakes of poisoned kid.

But all the fair sex of Kheibar were not so fickle as was Safia. Zeinab, who had lost her husband, as well as father and brothers, in the battle, planned a subtle revenge. She dressed a kid with dainty garnishing, and, having steeped it in poison, placed the dish with fair words before Mahomet at his evening repast. Accepting the gift, he took for himself his favourite piece, the shoulder, and distributed portions to Abu Bekr and other friends, including one called Bishr, who sat beside him. "Hold," cried Mahomet, as he spat forth the first mouthful, "sure this shoulder hath been poisoned." But Bishr had already swallowed part. Immediately he changed colour, and stirred neither hand nor foot until he died. The prophet also was seized with excruciating pains. As a cure, he had himself and all who had partaken with him freely cupped between the shoulders. When put on her defence, Zeinab answered bravely, "Thou hast inflicted grievous injuries on my people, and slain, as thou seest, my husband and my father. Therefore, said I within myself, If he be a prophet he will reject the gift, knowing that it is poisoned; but if only a pretender, we shall be rid of our troubler." According to most authorities, she was put to death. The poison was felt by Mahomet to his dying day.

Distribution of the booty.

The rest of Kheibar, taking warning by Kinâna's fate, capitulated, and so did the adjoining districts of Fadak and Wady al Cora. The plunder was immense,—dates and honey, oil and barley, treasure and jewels, flocks, herds, and camels,—an ample fulfilment of the prophecy. The movable spoil was distributed in the usual way. But the lands were otherwise disposed of. One-half was reserved as a crown domain, and, having been assessed at half the annual produce, was left in possession of the Jewish peasants. The rest was divided in freehold plots among the army. Mahomet had now an ample income at command. To each of his wives he made a liberal assignment,—so many measures annually of dates and barley. Nor were the poor forgotten. The remainder was appropriated for the entertainment of guests, the support of auxiliaries, and other purposes of state. The power of Mahomet no longer stood on spiritual resource alone, but on the substantial basis also of the sinews and thews of war.

Return of Abyssinian refugees.

On the way home Mahomet had the satisfaction of welcoming his cousin Jafar and the other Abyssinian exiles, who on their return went out to meet him. "I know not," said Mahomet on this occasion, "which delighteth me the most, the conquest of Kheibar or the return of Jafar." The army, no less pleased, acceded cheerfully to his proposal that their returning comrades should share equally with them in the spoil of Kheibar.

Marriage with Omm Habîba: ætat. 60.

On his return to Medina, Mahomet there took to himself Omm Habîba, thus consummating the marriage which the Negus had contracted for him in Abyssinia.

THE KÁABA, AS IT NOW STANDS, AT THE TIME OF PILGRIMAGE.

CHAPTER XXVII.

THE FULFILLED PILGRIMAGE. A.D. 629. A.H. VII. ÆTAT. 60.

THE remainder of the Seventh year of the Hegira, that is, the autumn and winter of 628 A.D., was spent by Mahomet at Medina. Several expeditions were undertaken under different leaders. With an occasional reverse, these were upon the whole successful. Some reached remote places, and though none was of any lasting importance, they continued to extend the name of Mahomet, and to bring him into relations, hostile or friendly, with surrounding and even distant tribes.

Expeditions in autumn and winter, A.D. 628.

The month at length came round when, according to the treaty of Hodeibia, Mahomet might revisit Mecca and fulfil the ceremonies of the Lesser Pilgrimage. The cavalcade set out two thousand in number. As stipulated, they bore only a sword apiece, with bow and arrows. But a heavy reserve of armour, in case of treachery, was carried separately, and deposited outside the sacred boundary. Sixty camels, to be slain as victims, were driven in front.

Mahomet sets out on Lesser Pilgrimage, February 629. A.H. VII.

At Mecca a singular scene was now to be enacted. When the pilgrims drew near, the Coreish, as it had been arranged, withdrew with their families from the city, and left it wholly empty. They climbed the heights of the overhanging hill, and there, from their tents, watched with curious eye the entrance of the prophet as he marched at the head of the long procession wending its way through the approaches of the Káaba. Seven years had passed since the exiles had seen their native valley, and now with quickened step they hastened forward as the sacred Temple rose in view, shouting the accustomed cry, *Labbeik! Labbeik!* Still mounted on his camel, Mahomet approached the Káaba, touched the Black stone reverently with his staff, and made the seven circuits round the holy house. Just then, the chief who led his camel broke out loudly with some warlike and defiant verses. "Gently," said Mahomet, reproving him. "Say rather, *There is no God but the Lord! It is He that hath upholden His servant, and exalted His people.* Alone hath He discomfited the Confederated hosts." The great concourse took up his words, shouting them aloud as they ran round about the Káaba, till the mighty sound reverberating, rang round the valley. The circuits completed, Mahomet adjourned to the adjoining eminences of Safa and Merwa, riding seven times from one to the other, according to the ancient custom. The victims were now drawn up in line and sacrificed. Then he shaved his head. And with this ended the ceremonies of the Lesser Pilgrimage. On the morrow, Mahomet again repaired to the Káaba, and ascended the interior chamber. Notwithstanding that the temple was still garnished with emblems of idolatry, Bilâl, mounting

Coreish withdraw while Mahomet performs pilgrimage.

the roof, summoned the Moslems with the usual cry to mid-day prayer; and there, under the shadow of the ancient house, the service was led by Mahomet in the same form as in the Mosque at Medina.

Mahomet warned by the Coreish to depart.

While at Mecca, Mahomet lived in a tent of leather pitched for him near the Káaba, and he entered into friendly converse with several of the citizens who ventured down from the heights into the valley. Nor was he deterred either by his sacred errand or by advancing years from seeking on this occasion another wife. This was Meimûna, a young widowed lady; she was sister-in-law to his uncle Abbas, through whom the marriage was negotiated. But the time was short. Already the three days stipulated had expired, when a deputation was sent by the Coreish to request that according to agreement he should depart. "And what harm," answered Mahomet, "if ye allow me to stay a little longer and celebrate my nuptials amongst you, and make for the guests a feast of which ye also might partake?" "Nay," said the chiefs, "of any food of thine we have no need. Withdraw from hence." So Mahomet departed, and by night-time not one of the pilgrims was left behind. The first stage on the homeward journey was Sarif, eight miles off; and there Mahomet received his bride, who was conducted to him by his servant on a camel. Early in the morning the march was resumed, and the pilgrim band journeyed back to Medina. Meimûna survived Mahomet fifty years, and was by her desire buried on the same spot where the prophet had welcomed her as his bride. This was Mahomet's last marriage. He had now in his harem ten wives; but one died before him, so that the number

Marriage with Meimûna.

was then reduced to nine, or, including slave-girls, eleven. He thus took large advantage of his special privilege. Other believers are limited by law to four free wives, though they may take for concubines as many bondmaids as they choose.

Conversion of Khâlid and Amru.

Mahomet carried with him to Medina Meimûna's sister, the widow of his uncle Hamza. Another sister was the mother of Khâlid the warrior who at Ohod had turned the battle against the Moslems. Not long after his aunt's marriage, Khâlid repaired to Medina, and joined the cause of Islam. Amru, a chief of almost equal influence, shortly followed, and several other leading men. Thus the position of Mahomet gained daily. A bold stroke might put an end to the struggle that had so long distracted Mecca. A *coup d'état* was fast becoming possible.

CHAPTER XXVIII.

BATTLE OF MUTA. A.D. 629. A.H. VIII. ÆTAT. 61.

DURING the summer and autumn of the Eighth year of the Hegira, the arms of Mahomet were again engaged in many small expeditions, and as before with varying results. Most of these were crowned with success, but some came to a disastrous end, and one or two parties were entirely cut up. The autumn was marked by a heavier campaign. Some tribes towards the Syrian border showed signs of hostility, and a messenger on his way to Bostra was put to death by the chief of Maâb, or Mûta. To avenge the affront, an army assembled at Medina three thousand strong. Placing a white banner in the hands of his friend Zeid, Mahomet bade him march to the spot where his envoy had been slain, with this command: "Call upon them to embrace Islam; if they refuse, then, in the name of the Lord draw the sword and fight." He accompanied the army as far as to the *Mount of Farewell* in the outskirts of the city, and thence as they passed onward before him, blessed them thus: "The Lord shield you from danger, and bring you back in peace, laden with spoil."

Campaign on Syrian border, Sept. 629.

Tidings of the coming army alarmed the Syrian

border, and a large force was quickly drawn together. Amongst them were some imperial cohorts commanded by an officer of distinction.

Roman army assembles.

The rumour grew as it spread, and Zeid was startled by the alarming report of the Kaiser himself being with a great army encamped at Maâb. A council was called, and for two days it was debated whether they should go forward or seek for fresh instructions. The counsels of the more ardent at last prevailed. "Is it in numbers," they cried, "or in the help of the Lord, that we put our trust? Victory or the martyr's crown, one or the other is secure." And so the army went on. When they had reached Belcâa, on the southern borders of the Dead Sea, they suddenly found themselves confronted by an enemy surpassing in numbers and equipment anything they had ever seen before.

Battle of Mûta.

Alarmed at the glittering array, they fell back on the village of Mûta. There finding advantageous ground, they stood, and resolved to give battle. The Roman phalanx, with clouds of Arab horse on either flank, moved steadily down upon them. Zeid, waving his white flag, led the Moslem columns on, till, fighting bravely at their head, he fell. Jáfar, cousin of Mahomet, second in command, seized the banner, and urged forward the attack. In token of death or victory, he maimed his horse, and fought on covered with wounds, until a Roman dealt him also the fatal blow. Then a Citizen, rescuing the standard, planted it on the ground, and as the line was giving way, shouted, "*Whither away, ye Moslems? come back!*" and so there was a temporary rally. The leadership being now vacant, a council of war hastily called together fixed their choice on the famous Khâlid, who forthwith assumed the

Defeat of the Moslem army.

command. But the chance of victory had passed away. The ranks were hopelessly broken, and the Romans in pursuit were already making havoc of the fugitives. To save the scattered columns from destruction taxed the genius of Khâlid to the utmost. By a series of skilful movements he drew off the shattered remains of the army to a safe retreat. But he dared not linger longer in the dangerous locality, and so, without further attempt to retrieve the day, he marched back to Medina. The people hooted and cast dust at them coming in, "as runaways who had fled when fighting for the Lord." "Nay," cried Mahomet, who had ridden out to meet them on his mule, carrying the little son of Jafar before him, "these are not runaways; they are men who will yet return to the fight, if the Lord will."

Khâlid saves the scattered remnants.

The reverse, and the loss of two such friends as Zeid and Jáfar, the brother of Aly, affected Mahomet deeply. Jáfar's widow tells us that she had just bathed and dressed her children, when the prophet entering embraced them, and burst into tears. She guessed the truth, and sobbed aloud. Returning home, he bade them send provisions to the bereaved household, "for none this day," said he, "will be prepared there." At the house of Zeid, the little daughter of his deceased friend rushed into his arms, crying bitterly. Mahomet, overcome, joined in her weeping. A bystander expostulated, "Why thus, O prophet?" He answered, "This is not the grief which is forbidden; this is nought but the yearning in the heart of friend for friend."

Mahomet visits families of Jáfar and Zeid.

The unruly people of the north, encouraged by the defeat, assembled in threatening numbers, and even talked of a descent upon Medina. Amru, the late convert, being kin to the

Syrian border restored to allegiance by Amru.

tribes in that quarter, was sent with an army to quell the rising, and restore the prestige of Islam on the Syrian frontier. He found the country all so hostile that he had to halt and send for reinforcements. These were despatched under Abu Obeida, to whom, although one of the oldest and chiefest of the Companions, Amru imperiously refused to surrender the command. Abu Obeida, who was of a milder temperament, yielded. It is interesting to notice in each of these commanders the same character already showing itself at this early period, as after the death of Mahomet marked their career in the Syrian wars. Thus strengthened, Amru again advanced, dispersed the hostile gatherings, confirmed the friendly tribes, and restored peace to the border.

Extending power and influence of Mahomet. A.D. 629. A.H. VIII.

Various other expeditions followed, ending successfully, and bringing spoil and captives, men and women, to the Moslems. The fame of Mahomet grew so rapidly, and the fear of his arms so widely spread abroad, that numerous tribes, even such as had been bitterly hostile hitherto, began now to send in their adhesion to the court of Medina. His courteous treatment of such deputations, and ready attention to their claims, the wisdom with which he composed their disputes, and the politic assignments of territory by which he rewarded early declaration in favour of Islam, made the name of Mahomet popular, as that of a great and generous Prince, throughout the Peninsula. And, moreover, the accession of so many tribes, all bound to furnish their contingents when so required, enabled him to call into the field an incomparably larger and more imposing force than he had heretofore aspired to lead, whenever the occasion might arise.

CHAPTER XXIX.

CONQUEST OF MECCA. JANUARY 630. A.H. VIII. ÆTAT. 61.

Beni Khozâa complain of breach of truce, Dec. 629 A.D. A.H. VIII.

THE truce of Hodeibia had been for two years in force, when a complaint of its infraction afforded Mahomet colourable pretext for attacking Mecca. Acting on the discretion given by the treaty, the Beni Khozâa and Beni Bekr, tribes inhabiting the neighbourhood of Mecca, had declared their adhesion, the former to the side of Mahomet, the latter to that of the Coreish. An old blood feud now broke out afresh between the two tribes, and the Beni Bekr, aided by a party of the Coreish in disguise, attacked the Khozâa by night and slew some of them. A deputation from the injured tribe hastened to Medina, spread their wrongs before the prophet, and demanded justice. The longed-for opportunity had come. Starting up, with his garments yet ungirded, Mahomet at once exclaimed, "If I help you not in like wise as if the wrong were mine own, let me never more be helped by the Lord! See ye not the rain pouring down from yonder cloud? Even so shall help descend upon the Beni Khozâa speedily."

The Coreish, learning the errand of the Khozâa, were alarmed. They despatched Abu Sofiân to Medina to protest against the charge; but he could get no response from Mahomet. At last, in despair, he stood up in the court of the great Mosque and cried, "Hearken, ye people, unto me! Peace and protection I guarantee for all." Whereupon the prophet made reply, "It is thou that sayest it, not one of us, O Abu Sofiân!" So he departed, rebuffed and in uncertainty. The Coreish perceived that they were in evil case, but they did not suspect how imminent the designs of Mahomet against them were.

Unsuccessful mission of Abu Sofiân.

In fact, Mahomet had already resolved on an immediate and grand attack upon his native city. The design, however, was kept secret by him even from his closest friends. Meanwhile, he busied himself in summoning his Bedouin allies to muster in strength at Medina, or at convenient points upon the road. But he held their destination hid, and to divert attention despatched a party of soldiers in another quarter. At the last moment he announced his project, but still enjoined the utmost caution, so that not a breath regarding it should transpire at Mecca. "O Lord!" he prayed, "let not any spy carry tidings to the Coreish. Blind their eyes, until that I come upon them suddenly and take them unawares!" Such was the petition offered up daily by him in the Mosque.

Preparations for attacking Mecca.

The army was the largest Medina had ever seen. Bedouin camps darkened the plain all round, and heavy contingents joined by the way, so that Mahomet now found himself at the head of ten thousand men. Zeinab and Omm Salma were his companions on the march, which was forced

Army marches, 1st Jan. 630 A.D. A.H. VIII.

with such rapidity that within a week he was but a single stage from Mecca. To strike terror into the rebellious city, ten thousand fires were kindled on the heights above the camp. So stealthy, quick, and unexpected was the movement, and the host so overwhelming, that the Coreish were panic-struck, and perceived at once the hopelessness of opposition. Abbâs, secretly apprized, had already joined the prophet on the march; and Abu Sofiân, opportunely met by him as he ventured forth to reconnoitre, was conducted to his Nephew's presence. *Out upon thee, Abu Sofiân!* exclaimed the prophet as the Coreishite chief drew near;—*hast thou not yet discerned that there is no God but the Lord alone?* "Noble and generous sire," he answered, "had there been any beside, he surely had been of some avail to me." *And dost thou not acknowledge me to be the Prophet of the Lord?* "Noble sire, as to this thing, there is still some hesitancy within." "Woe is thee!" cried Abbas; "it is no time for hesitancy this. Believe and testify the faith at the peril of thy neck!" It was indeed no time for idle pride or scruple, and so Abu Sofiân repeated the formula of belief in the Lord and in Mahomet as His prophet. The troops were already marshalling, and time was precious. "Haste thee to the city," said Mahomet to his great antagonist, now a suppliant at his feet;—"hasten, and say that none who taketh refuge in the house of Abu Sofiân shall be harmed this day; and whoso closeth the door of his house, the inmates thereof shall be safe." Hurrying away to his home, Abu Sofiân made proclamation in the words of Mahomet; and so, with few exceptions, the people fled every man to his house or to the Káaba.

Reaches neighbourhood of Mecca by forced marches.

Abu Sofiân, tendering submission, sent with peaceful message to Mecca.

The troops, marshalled in four columns, approached the city by as many different roads. Mahomet, with the Refugees, led by Abu Obeida, took the nearest way. The anxieties of a lifetime crowded into the moment. But as the city opened on the prophet's view, it was plain that his precautions had taken due effect; and so, bending low upon his camel, he offered thanksgiving to the Lord. Mercy and forbearance had been enjoined upon the leaders. The columns entered peaceably, all excepting that of Khâlid. The southern suburb, assigned to him, was inhabited by bitter opponents of the prophet. His battalion, composed of Bedouins difficult at any time to hold in hand, was saluted as it neared the place with a shower of arrows. The Bedouins, let loose, at once discomfited the enemy; and Khâlid, flushed with success and unmindful of his master's orders, pursued through the streets the fugitive Coreish. Eight-and-twenty were cut up, while Khâlid lost but two men. As Mahomet entered Mecca from the opposite side, his grateful sense was turned suddenly into concern as he caught sight of the gleam of swords. "What!" he cried in anger; "did not I give strict command that there should be no fighting?" The cause was explained, whereupon the prophet said, "What the Lord decreeth that is best."

Army enters the city in four columns.

Khâlid meets with opposition.

Mahomet then encamped his great host at the point where the valley opens out above the town. There his leathern tent was pitched, not far from the graves of Abu Tâlib and Khadîja. The chief banner was planted at his door. Assured now that the city, as it lay before him, was wholly at his will, he retired within his tent to rest, and ponder

Mahomet reposes in his tent.

over the accomplishment of that which had been the dream of his life.

But he did not long repose. Again mounting his camel, he reverently performed the worship of the Káaba. Pointing to the idols one by one that stood around it with his staff, he commanded them to be hewn down. *Truth hath come*, he cried aloud, in the words of the Coran, as the image of Hobal fell with a crash,—*Truth hath come, and Falsehood hath gone; for Falsehood verily vanisheth away.* Then calling for the key wherewith to open the door, he ascended the steps of the doorway, entered the Temple, and devoutly bowed himself therein. Returning to the elevated threshold, and catching hold of the rings attached to either side, he gazed in thankfulness on the thronging multitude below. "Here," he cried, naming the hereditary Guardian of the temple, "here, take back the key, to be kept a perpetual charge by thee and thy posterity. And thou, Abbâs" (turning to his uncle), "I confirm thee in the giving of drink to pilgrims from out of the well Zem-zem. It is no mean office that I now give unto thee."

Worships at Káaba, and destroys idols.

Sura xvii. 82.

The idols destroyed, and the figures painted on the walls of the Káaba obliterated, worship was performed by the multitude in the court of the Káaba after the ritual of the great Mosque at Medina. A crier was then sent through the city, proclaiming that no idol should be left in any house that was not broken in pieces. A party was at the same time deputed to repair the pillars marking the limits of the sacred environs. Mahomet thus gave proof that while utterly uprooting idolatry from the land, he was equally bent on upholding the sanctity of Mecca and

Mahomet's love for Mecca.

the obligation of its worship. He wôn the hearts of the people by his ardent declaration of love for their city. "Thou art the choicest spot upon earth to me," he said, "and the most delectable. If thy people had not cast me forth, I never had forsaken thee!" The men of Medina now expressed their fear that he would not return to Medina as his home. But he speedily reassured them. "The Lord forbid that," he answered, with the strongest asseveratión; "where ye live, there will I live, and there also shall I die."

Certain citizens proscribed.

From the general amnesty Mahomet excepted ten or twelve persons, but the greater number even of these he pardoned. Two men were proscribed for the ruffianly attack on his daughter Zeinab, but one of them escaped, and was eventually forgiven. Two others were renegade Moslems, who, having shed blood at Medina, had fled to Mecca. They were now executed, together with a singing girl belonging to one of them, who had annoyed the prophet with her satires. An apostate scribe, Abu Sarh,[1] to whom the prophet used to dictate passages of the Coran, was spared, though unwillingly, at the entreaty of his friends. Ikrima, son of Abu Jahl, and Safwân, a chief of note, eluded the pursuit of Khâlid. Reaching the sea-shore, they were on the point of embarking, when, on the assurance of pardon, they were persuaded to return. Hind, who had compassed the death of Hamza, and another singing girl, escaped death by opportune submission. Thus of the whole number only four were actually put to death, and these (with the exception only, one might say, of the singing girl) with perhaps sufficient reason.

The magnanimity with which Mahomet treated a

[1] He was foster-brother to Othmân, and we hear more of him under his Caliphate. See 'Annals of the Early Caliphate,' p. 298.

people who had so long hated and rejected him, had its reward. The whole city espoused his cause. There were no dissentients here, nor any disaffected citizens, as there had been at Medina; and shortly after we find two thousand of the Coreish fighting loyally by his side.

Magnanimity of Mahomet and adhesion of Meccans.

Parties were sent throughout the surrounding country to destroy the images of Al Ozza and Manât, and other tutelary shrines. This was effected for the most part peaceably. But Khâlid, giving thus early proof of his sanguinary temper, encouraged his Bedouins to put to death some prisoners of a tribe that had offered opposition. On receiving intelligence of the mishap, Mahomet raised his hands to heaven and cried, "O Lord, I am innocent in Thy sight of that which Khâlid hath done!" and, to prove the sincerity of his regret, he sent Aly to make compensation for the slain and to return the plunder.

Idols in neighbourhood destroyed.

Severity of Khâlid disavowed by Mahomet.

By the conquest of Mecca, Mahomet achieved a position from which it was now possible to impose his faith upon the whole Peninsula. Lord of the Káaba, a shrine worshipped by nearly the entire Arabian nation, he was able now to dictate the conditions of its worship, and thus to mould the national faith. It remained but that the office of the prophet should be accredited by the power of the conqueror; and for conquest there was everything in Mahomet's favour. Master of Mecca and Medina, he possessed as such a powerful following among the Bedouins of Central Arabia; and with them to support him, supremacy throughout the Peninsula was assured. But there was rough work for him yet to go through before reaching the sovereign object of his ambition.

Review of position now attained.

CHAPTER XXX.

BATTLE OF HONEIN—SIEGE OF TAYIF.

JANUARY—MARCH 630 A.D. A.H. VIII.

Hostile designs of Beni Hawâzin.

A STORM that lowered in the east cut short the stay of Mahomet at Mecca. There was no mistaking his iconoclastic aim, and Tâyif trembled for its faith and liberties. This city, 60 or 70 miles east of Mecca, was the centre of a local worship, to which the great Bedouin clan of the Beni Hawâzin were devoted. In an early offensive movement (as it would seem to them) lay their only chance of safety, and so they assembled in great force on the road leading from Tâyif to Mecca. Having provided for the government of his native city—an obligation now devolving on him as its conqueror—Mahomet marshalled his troops, and marched forth to meet the gathering foe. His army was swelled by a contingent of the Coreish to 12,000 men. The array of tribes, each with a banner waving at its head, was so imposing that Abu Bekr broke forth in admiration, saying that they should not this day be worsted, at any rate by reason of the smallness of their numbers. Mahomet smiled complacently, but afterwards saw reason to reproach himself for falling into the temptation of so vainglorious an attitude.

The Beni Hawâzin halted in the valley of Honein,

between Tâyif and Mecca. Their women and children, herds and flocks, were posted in the rear, to render defeat, as it were, impossible. As Mahomet approached, their chief, Mâlik, masked his forces in a steep and narrow defile leading into the valley. At early dawn the Moslem army was in motion. Mounted on his white mule, Mahomet rode in the rear. The vanguard, led by Khâlid, were already within the pass, when suddenly the Beni Hawâzin sprang from their ambuscade. Staggered by the onset, column after column fell back, and choked the narrow pass. Panic spread, and the troops turned and fled. "Whither away? Return, return!" cried Mahomet, as troop after troop hurried past him. But the rush and crush went on, camels jostled one another wildly, and the prophet's voice was lost amid the din. Just then the Medina column bore down the narrow valley in the common rout, and Mahomet seeing it, bade Abbâs, who had a stentorian voice, to shout, "*Men of Medina! Ye men of the Pledge of the Tree!*" The words touched a chord in their heart, and they cried, "*Yâ Labbeik!* Yes, here we are!" A hundred of these planted themselves across the gorge; and thus relieved of pressure, the troops behind rallied and returned to the fight. Mahomet, climbing an eminence, watched the struggle, which for a time was doubtful. "Now is the furnace heated!" he cried excitedly; "I am the prophet that lieth not, the seed of Abd al Muttalib!" Then catching up a handful of gravel he cast it at the enemy. "*Ruin seize them! I swear they are discomfited!*" he shouted eagerly, as he saw them wavering. "By the Lord of the Káaba, they yield! The Lord hath cast fear into their hearts!" The moment was

Battle of Honein. Feb. 630. A.H. VIII.

Moslem army gives way.

Enemy routed.

critical, but in the end the enemy turned and fled. The rout was complete, and so fierce the pursuit that some of the women and children even were killed, an atrocity strictly forbidden by Mahomet.

And their families captured.

Mâlik taking his stand at the further end of the valley, covered the flight of his broken forces. But the women and children, the camp, with herds and flocks and long strings of camels, all fell into the conqueror's hands. The prisoners, 6000 in number, were placed in the adjoining valley of Jierrâna, and guarded there while the army went on to Tâyif; for Mahomet felt sure that the vanquished tribe would return and open negotiations for the release of their families.

Victory ascribed to heavenly aid.

The victory, though complete, was not gained without considerable loss. Ten of Mahomet's immediate followers fell; but the auxiliaries exposed to the first brunt of the attack suffered the most; two tribes were almost annihilated, and for them Mahomet prayed that the Lord would recompense them for their calamities. In the passages which treat of this battle, the reverse sustained at the outset is attributed to the vainglorious trust in their numbers with which the army set out from Mecca, while the eventual success is ascribed to unseen hosts sent down from heaven to fight for the faith:—

Sura ix.

> Verily the LORD hath assisted you in many battle-fields, and notably in the day of HONEIN, when ye rejoiced in the multitude of your army. But the multitude did not in any wise benefit you. The earth with all its spaciousness became too strait for you. And so ye turned your backs and fled. Then after that, the Lord caused His peace to descend on His Prophet and on the Faithful, and sent down Hosts which ye saw not, and thereby punished the unbelievers. And such is the end of them that disbelieve.

The army, having left a detachment at Jierrâna, passed on to the attack of Tâyif. But the battlements were strong, the city well provisioned, and a plentiful supply of water within its walls. The Moslems pitched at first too near. Showers of arrows, like flights of locusts, darkened the air. Twelve men were killed; many were wounded, and amongst them a son of Abu Bekr. The camp was therefore retired to a spot out of range, and there tents were pitched for Omm Salma and Zeinab, who had followed their lord through all the dangers of the way. On a spot between the two, Mahomet performed the daily prayers, and there eventually rose the great Mosque of Tâyif. A southern tribe, familiar with the use of besieging engines, built a battering-ram, which was run up against the walls; but the besieged poured down heated iron, and set it thus on fire. At last, as the only means of bringing the place to terms, Mahomet gave command to cut down and burn to their roots the vines of the famous vineyards surrounding the town. The citizens expostulated against the wanton injury, as opposed to the laws of war; and orders were issued to stay the merciless destruction. But in place of it, proclamation was made of freedom to all slaves that might desert. Twenty escaped, much to the chagrin of the garrison, and fought thereafter in the ranks of their liberators.

Siege laid to Tâyif, February 630 A.D. A.H. VIII.

Half a month passed thus without effect. The army became impatient to share the spoil in store for them at Jierrâna. A council of war was held, and Mahomet asked the leaders what they thought of this stubborn city. "A fox in its hole," answered an astute old chief; "sit long enough before the hole, and ye will catch it; depart, and it will not

Siege raised.

harm you." A dream of Mahomet enforced the adage, and so the army raised the siege and marched back to Jierrâna.

While arrangements were in progress there for the distribution of the captives and the prey, a female made her way into the prophet's presence. It was the daughter of his nurse Halîma, who reminded him of her attendance on him as a little girl, when he was nurtured in her family. She was received affectionately and dismissed with a present. Emboldened by her kind reception, the whole clan pressed their claim. Among the prisoners, they said, were his foster mothers and his foster sisters,—"they that have nursed thee and fondled thee in their bosoms; and now thou art risen to this dignity. Be gracious unto us, even as the Lord hath been gracious unto thee!" He was moved at their entreaty, and persuaded the army to give up the captives without ransom.

Hawâzin captives set at liberty.

Returning to his tent, an impatient throng surrounded him, crying out, "Distribute to us the spoil, the camels and the flocks!" So rudely did they jostle, that he was driven to take refuge under a tree, and his mantle was torn from his shoulders. "O man, return to me my mantle," said Mahomet, extricating himself with some difficulty from the press; "for I swear that if the sheep and camels were as many as the trees of the forest in number, I would divide them all amongst you." Then plucking from his camel's hump a hair, he held it up and said, "Even to this I would keep back nought but the Fifth, and even that I will divide amongst you." They were pacified, and Mahomet went on his way.

Mahomet mobbed by discontented followers.

The booty was then distributed. Over and above their proper share, Mahomet gave princely gifts, to gain the hearts of the leading men of Mecca and of the Bedouin chiefs, not long ago his sworn enemies; to some a hundred camels, and to some fifty. Though taken from the prophet's Fifth, these largesses to new and doubtful converts gave umbrage to his veteran followers. The citizens of Medina especially, began to say that, now joined by his own people, he had forgotten them. This coming to the prophet's ears, he called the murmurers to him, and reminded them of the benefits, temporal and spiritual, he had conferred upon them. After enumerating these, he asked, "Is it not so?" and paused for a reply. "It is indeed," they answered with one voice. "Nay, but," continued Mahomet, "ye might have said to me, and said truly,—*Thou camest to us rejected, and we bare thee witness; a fugitive, and we took thee in; destitute, and we fed thee.* Why are ye disturbed because I have sought to gain these men unto the faith in the which ye are already stablished? Are ye not satisfied to leave the flocks and the herds to them, while ye carry back with you the prophet of the Lord? Nay, I will never leave you. The Lord bless the men of Medina, their sons, and their sons' sons for evermore." They were melted, the tears ran down upon their beards, and they cried out with one voice, "Yea, we are well satisfied, O prophet, with our lot!" Nevertheless, a grave misdemeanour had been committed by those who found fault with the distribution, and a passage was accordingly revealed bearing a divine reprimand for the same. The legitimate recipients of public charity had before been

Largesses to Meccan and Bedouin chiefs,

cause discontent among citizens of Medina.

Sura ix. 62.

laid down as the "poor and needy, the wayfarer," and certain other deserving classes. It was needful for Mahomet now to justify his own action in stepping beyond these limits; and so a new class is added in this passage as proper objects of public gifts, namely, "those whose hearts are to be gained over to the faith."

Mahomet performs Lesser Pilgrimage, March 630 A.D.

The distribution ended, Mahomet took upon him the pilgrim vows, and fulfilled the rites of the Lesser Pilgrimage at Mecca. But he made no stay there. Returning to his camp at Jierrâna, he took thence the direct route home to Mecca.

Annual pilgrimage, April 630 A.D. Dzul Hijj VIII.

The Annual pilgrimage followed shortly after, but Mahomet did not go up to it. The ceremonies were presided over by the governor, Attâb, a youthful chief of the Coreish, whom the prophet had appointed as his vice-gerent to the charge of Mecca. Idolaters were still allowed freely to mingle with believers in performance of the rites.

CHAPTER XXXI.

MARY AND HER SON. A.D. 630, 631. A.H. VIII.—X. ÆTAT. 61, 62.

Death of Zeinab, Mahomet's daughter.

In the Ninth year of the Hegira, Mahomet lost his daughter Zeinab, who had never recovered the ill-treatment she suffered on her escape from Mecca. Omm Kolthum, whom Othmân married after Rockeya's death, had also died, so that of his children Fatima at this time alone survived. He was now for a brief space to be solaced by another child.

Mary bears a son, April 630 A.D. End of A.H. VIII.

A singular fortune elevated Mary, the Coptic bondmaid, to a dignity which her beauty alone could not have secured for her. She and her sister professed originally the Christian faith, but no doubt they had by this time gone over to Islam. A garden-house in the suburbs of the city was prepared for Mary, and there, in the summer season, she used to receive the visits of the prophet. In course of time she gave promise of becoming a mother, and the aged Salma, who had long before attended the birth of Khadîja's children, was now engaged to perform the same office for Mary. Shortly after the return of the army from Tâyif, she gave birth to a son. Mahomet's joy was great. He called the child's name Ibrahîm, and on the seventh day sacrificed a kid; he also shaved his head, and distributed silver among the poor to the weight of the hair, which then was burned. He would daily visit the house of the nurse, embrace the infant, and kiss it fondly. But his wives were jealous at Mary's fortune. As the child grew, Mahomet carried it once to Ayesha, and bade her to mark how like it was to himself. "I do not see it," said Ayesha, who would gladly have put her husband out of conceit with the little Ibrahîm. "What!" rejoined he, "canst thou not see the likeness, and how fair and well-looking he is?" "Yes," she answered, "and so would be any other infant that did drink as much milk as he." A flock of milch goats was kept for the child's special service.

But the jealousy of Mary's "Sisters" betrayed itself in a more serious way. It happened that Haphsa went to visit her father on the day when her own turn came round. Returning unexpectedly, she surprised Mary with the prophet in her own apartment. The affront was aggravated by the servile station of her rival. To escape exposure and appease his indignant spouse, Mahomet begged of her to keep the matter secret, promising to forego the company of Mary altogether. But Haphsa did not care to hide her wrong; she told it all to Ayesha, who boiled with indignation at the shameful tale. The scandal spread, and Mahomet soon found himself received by all his wives with coldness and reserve.

Scandal in Mahomet's harem.

As in the affair of Zeinab, so here also a heavenly message interposed. The oracle disallowed the promise to refrain from Mary's company, chided both the chief offenders for insubordination, and hinted at the possibility of the whole harem being

Mahomet displeased with his wives.

divorced in favour of other consorts more complacent. Having delivered the warning, he withdrew from the society of his wives, and for a whole month lived alone with Mary. Omar and Abu Bekr were mortified at the scandal, and at the desertion of their daughters for a menial concubine. Mahomet at last relented. Gabriel, he said, had spoken well of Haphsa, and desired that he should receive her back. So he forgave them, and returned to their apartments as before. Here is the heavenly message :—

> O Prophet! why hast thou forbidden thyself that which the Lord hath made lawful unto thee, desiring to please thy wives? . . . Verily the Lord hath sanctioned the recalling of your oaths. . . . Now the Prophet had entrusted one of his wives with a certain secret; and when she disclosed it to another, and the Lord revealed this unto him— ; so when he had acquainted her therewith, she said, *Who told thee this?* He answered, He told it me, the Knowing and the Wise. If ye both turn to the Lord with repentance (for ver.ly the hearts of you both have swerved), well. But if ye side with each other against him, verily God is his Master. . . .
>
> Haply, the Lord, if he divorce you, will give him in your stead Wives better than ye are, submissive unto God, believing, pious, repentant, fasting,—both Women previously married, and Virgins.[1]

Sura lxvi.

There is surely no grotesquer utterance by way of a "revelation" in the "sacred books of the East" than this strange passage, and yet it has been gravely read all these ages, and is still read, by the Moslem, both in public and private, as part of the Divine (and, as most part hold it to be, the "eternal")

This passage still read as part of Coran.

[1] The Sura, which is a curiosity from beginning to end, concludes with a warning allusion to two wicked women, who, though the wives of good men, Noah and Lot, were condemned to hell, and to two good women, the wife of Pharaoh and the Virgin Mary, who were examples of virtue and piety.

Coran. It is a relief to turn to a more edifying passage in the prophet's life.

Sickness and death of Ibrahîm, summer 631 A.D. A.H. X.

The infant Ibrahîm having now reached the age of sixteen months, fell sick, and it was soon seen that he would not long survive. The child was laid in the shade of a palm-grove near the house of his nurse. There Mary with her sister tended the dying infant, and there too was Mahomet bowed down with sorrow. Perceiving that his little son would soon pass away, he folded him in his arms and sobbed. They tried to comfort him, and said that he had counselled others to moderate their grief. "Not so," he answered as he hung over the expiring child; "it is not this that I forbade, but wailing and fulsome laudation of the dead. Ibrahîm, O Ibrahîm! If it were not that the promise is faithful, and the hope of Resurrection sure, and that the last of us shall rejoin the first, I would have grieved for thee with a sorrow sorer even than this!" But the spirit had passed away; so he laid the little body down, saying, "The remainder of the days of his nursing shall be fulfilled in Paradise." Then he comforted Mary and her sister, and bade them, now that the child was gone, to be silent and resigned. When the little bier was ready, Mahomet followed it to the burying-ground. He prayed there, as his custom was, and lingered at the grave after it had been levelled over. He then had water sprinkled upon the ground, and observing some unevenness, he smoothed it with his hand, remarking, "When ye do this thing, do it carefully. It cannot injure the dead, neither can it profit, but the same giveth comfort to the living."

In gratitude for her services he gave the nurse a parcel of ground planted over with date trees.

CHAPTER XXXII.

CAMPAIGN OF TEBUK—SUBMISSION OF TAYIF.

A.D. 630. A.H. IX.

AFTER the battle of Honein no serious fighting took place during what remained of the prophet's life. Expeditions were, indeed, frequently sent forth to humble defiant tribes, and to punish those that were defaulting in their tithe or tribute, or otherwise rebellious. But none of them deserves special mention excepting only the campaign of Tebûk, which is remarkable not merely for the unprecedented size of the army, but still more for the denunciations of Mahomet against the malingerers.

No more serious fighting.

Alarmed at the repeated incursion of Moslem bands, and the rapid growth of the new power which threatened southern Syria, the Byzantine court directed the tribes in that quarter to assemble for its protection. Rumours of the movement reached Medina in an exaggerated shape. Multitudes, they heard, were gathering under the Roman eagles, and the vanguard was already at Belcâa. Mahomet resolved to meet the danger promptly, and although the season was sultry and water on the journey scarce, he issued peremptory summons that all within

Campaign towards Syrian frontier, Sept. 630 A.D. A.H. IX.

reasonable distance should join the army of Mecca and Medina in an expedition northward. But the Bedouins, ever loose and fickle in their loyalty, hung back, and many even of the Citizens shrank from the exposure and hardships of the way. They pleaded inability, or some such frivolous excuse. The plea of inability, when urged by the men of Medina, to whom Mahomet owed so much, was generally accepted; but coming from the Bedouins it was altogether disallowed.

Malingering Bedouins and Citizens.

On the other hand, the utmost zeal pervaded the ranks of loyal and earnest Moslems. Tithes and offerings poured in from every quarter. The leading Companions vied with one another in the costliness of their gifts. From these sources a great army was equipped, and carriage provided for the indigent who longed to share in the merit, haply also in the spoils, of the campaign. Numbers of these for whom no such provision could be made, retired weeping from the Mosque in front of which the troops were marshalling, and their memory is embalmed in tradition by the name of *The Weepers.* When all was ready the army encamped outside the city. Abdallah pitched his camp hard by, but at the last he was allowed to remain with his men behind. Aly also was left in charge of the prophet's family, with the view also to check any rising of disaffection that might transpire during his absence from the city.

Zeal of loyal followers.

The force, with all these drawbacks, was by far the largest which in the experience or memory of the Arabs had ever before been set in motion. The numbers are set down at 30,000, of whom 10,000 were cavalry. After a hot and thirsty march of between two and three hundred miles on the road to Syria, the army halted at Tebûk, where were shade and

March to Tebûk.

water in abundance. But the rumour of Roman invasion had by this time died away, and so Mahomet contented himself with sending forward a column to Dûma under Khâlid, while at his standing camp he received the adhesion of such Jewish and Christian settlements as bordered on the Ælanitic Gulf. John, prince of Ayla, appeared, having on his forehead a golden cross. The prophet entertained him courteously, and granted a treaty guaranteeing his people in the secure profession of their faith on payment of a yearly tribute. He was then presented with a striped mantle and honourably dismissed. Similar engagements were entered into with the Jewish settlements in the vicinity. And so, having halted in this distant quarter for several weeks, the army returned after a prolonged absence to Medina. The raid made by Khâlid as far as Dûma was entirely successful. He surprised the city, captured the prince, and marched back laden with booty. The captive chief, wearing a golden cross, and clad in brocade, was an object of admiration to the simple citizens of Medina. The inducements to embrace Islam proved too strong for his faith. He surrendered the Gospel for the Coran, and was admitted to the terms of a favoured ally.

John, prince of Ayla.

Return to Medina.

Prince of Dûma embraces Islam.

Many of those who had stayed behind were now forward to exculpate themselves from the heavy charge of malingering. Mahomet reserved his reproaches for a special Sura (the latest in the chronological order of the Coran), in which the vials of his wrath are discharged upon them :—

Malingerers reprimanded.

Had it been plunder near at hand and an easy journey, they had surely followed thee. But the way seemed long unto them. They will swear unto thee by the Lord, *Had*

Sura ix.

we been able, we would surely have gone forth with you. They destroy their own souls, for God knoweth they are liars. The Lord pardon thee; for why didst thou (O Mahomet) give them leave, until that thou hadst distinguished the truthful amongst them from the liars? . . . Verily they thought to stir up sedition aforetime, and they disturbed thine affairs until that the Truth came. . . . Among them there is that saith, *Give me leave to remain behind, and lead me not into temptation.* What! have they not fallen into temptation already? Verily Hell shall compass the Unbelievers round about. They said, *Go not forth to war in the heat.* Say, The fire of Hell is a fiercer heat, if they but understood. Wherefore they shall laugh little and weep much for that which they have wrought.

The Bedouins are specially reprobated as an ignorant, fickle, and stiff-necked race, that watched but the chances of fortune. "Turn from them. They are an abomination. Their resting-place shall be hell-fire." Those that had scoffed at the faith, and likewise at such as had aided the campaign by their contributions, are bitterly denounced. Nevermore shall they be allowed the opportunity of going forth to fight. "Neither do thou ever" (so runs the heavenly oracle) "pray over any one of them that may die, nor stand over his grave. These reject God and His prophet. They shall die as transgressors."

Such was the indignant rebuke pronounced upon the lukewarm and disaffected citizens. Some whose loyalty was beyond dispute were pardoned on presentation of costly offerings, whereby they were "cleansed and purified." Others were treated with greater severity, and notably three of the worst offenders. These last were placed under a ban, and debarred from intercourse even with their wives and families. Fifty days passed thus, and their lives became intolerable. At last the oracle relented:—

Punishment of certain malingerers.

Verily the Lord is reconciled unto the Prophet and the Citizens who followed him in the hour of difficulty, after that the hearts of a part of them had nearly swerved. . . And He is likewise reconciled unto the Three,—they that stayed behind, until the earth with all its spaciousness became straitened unto them, and their own souls were straitened within them, and they saw no refuge from the Lord otherwise than by fleeing unto Him. Then He turned unto them; for the Lord is easy to be reconciled and merciful. Sura ix.

Shortly after this, Abdallah died. Considering his persistent opposition, Mahomet had upon the whole treated him throughout with much forbearance. He even followed the bier of this once powerful antagonist, and prayed over his grave, thus recognizing him as a true believer. Of the disaffected party, there remained now no one of rank or influence whom Mahomet had reason to fear. The faction had ceased. Such as had been disloyal—the "Hypocrites" of the Coran—now embraced the cause with outward heartiness. The authority of the prophet at Medina was thenceforward sole and unquestioned.

Death of Abdallah ibn Obey.

About this time the city of Tâyif tendered its submission. For ten months the people had been harried by bands of Bedouins, who at the instigation of Mahomet carried on a predatory warfare against them. Cattle were cut off at pasture, and no man's life was safe beyond the city walls. In their extremity they sent a deputation to Medina. It was kindly received. A tent was pitched for them by the Great Mosque, and there, morning and evening, they were instructed in the requirements of Islam. The first demand was that every trace of idolatry should be removed. As for themselves, submitted the strangers, they were ready to give up their tutelary idol; but

Embassy from Tâyif, Dec. 630 A.D. A.H. IX.

its immediate demolition, they urged, would alarm the people. "Spare it," they said, "for three years, and the citizens, by that time well instructed, will then readily consent." Mahomet refused. Two years, one year, six months, were pleaded for, but all in vain. "The grace of one month might surely be allowed." The prophet was firm. The idol and Islam could not for a single day exist together. Again, they sought to be excused from the obligation of daily prayers; for so hostile were the people, that but recently a convert had been shot at and killed while performing his devotions on the roof of his house at Tâyif. They also begged that some one might be sent to destroy the idol for them. "As for the demolition of the idol with your own hands," answered Mahomet, "that I will dispense with; but the other is a matter of life and death, for *Religion without Prayer were naught.*" A Companion of note, kin to the tribe, was commissioned by Mahomet to destroy the idol. Wielding an axe, and surrounded by a guard of his relatives, he ruthlessly attacked the great image, and amid the wailing of the women hewed it to the ground. Tâyif was the last stronghold that held out against the authority of Mahomet. It is also the only spot where we read of the fate of an idol exciting the sympathy of the people. Everywhere else the images seem to have been destroyed by the people themselves without a pang.

Submission of Tâyif.

CHAPTER XXXIII.

PILGRIMAGE UNDER THE PRESIDENCY OF ABU BEKR—DECLARATION OF WAR AGAINST HEATHEN TRIBES. A.D. 631. A.H. IX.

THE closing month of the Arabian year, which is also the month of pilgrimage, again drew nigh. At the annual pilgrimage which took place shortly after the taking of Mecca, Mahomet had not appeared. The reason, no doubt, was that a vast proportion of the devotees were heathen; and the same cause kept him away on this occasion also. But he resolved that it should be the last festival desecrated by the worship of idolaters. He was now strong enough to banish heathenism for ever from the Holy city. When thus purged, then, but not till then, the solemn rites might be observed by him without compromising his prophetic office. This year, accordingly, the presidency, as chief of the pilgrimage, was given to Abu Bekr, who set out upon the journey with a small caravan of three hundred followers.

Annual pilgrimage, March 631 A.D. A.H. IX.

Presided over by Abu Bekr.

Shortly after his departure the oracle spoke, and a passage was promulgated to carry out the object Mahomet had in view. It is called the *Discharge*, because it discharges the prophet, after the lapse of four months, from all obligations

Aly sent to proclaim the Discharge, or war against idolaters.

towards the heathen tribes. These are everywhere to be fought against until they submit and embrace Islam; and never again must idolaters dare to approach the Káaba. Bearing this declaration, Aly was despatched in haste after the caravan, with the commission to recite the Divine behest in the ears of all the people. Accordingly, at the close of the pilgrimage, on the great day of sacrifice, Aly read before the multitude that crowded around him in the vale of Mina the "Discharge," of which the following verses will explain the drift:—

A DISCHARGE by God and His Apostle, in respect of the heathen with whom ye have entered into treaty. Go to and fro in the earth securely in the four months to come. . .

Sura ix.

And an ANNOUNCEMENT from God and His Apostle unto the people on the day of the Greater Pilgrimage,[1] that God is discharged from liability to the heathen, and His Prophet in like wise, . . . excepting such of them as ye have entered into treaty with, and who thereafter have not failed you in any matter, nor helped any one against you. Unto these fulfil ye their engagements.

Then, when the forbidden months are elapsed, fight against the heathen, wheresoever ye may find them. Take them captive, besiege them, and lay in wait for them in every ambush. But if they repent and set up prayer, and give tithes, then leave them alone. And if any ask a guarantee, give it him until he shall have heard the word of God; then convey him back again to his place of security.

O ye Faithful! Verily the Heathen are unclean. Wherefore let them not again approach the Holy temple after this year.

Having finished the recitation, Aly expounded the

[1] The *Annual* Pilgrimage, still held on the 8th to the 10th of Dzul Hijj, the last month of the Arabian calendar; and distinguished (as already explained) from the *Lesser* Pilgrimage, which with fewer ceremonies is performed at any period of the year.

edict thus:—"I am commanded to declare unto you that no unbeliever shall enter paradise. After this year no idolater shall perform the pilgrimage, nor shall any one circumambulate the Holy house unclothed. Whosoever hath a treaty, it shall be respected until its term expire. Four months are given to the tribes, that they may return to their homes in security. Thereafter the obligations of the prophet cease and do determine."

Aly explains the edict.

The vast concourse listened peaceably. Then they departed every man to his own home, publishing throughout the peninsula the inexorable ordinance which they had heard from the lips of Aly. To the utmost bounds of Arabia, wheresoever the worship of the Káaba prevailed, idolatry was doomed, and Islam henceforth alone was to be the nation's faith.

Concourse of pilgrims disperse.

Side by side with this deliverance is another affecting Jews and Christians. For some years the leaves of the oracle, which used to teem with testimonies to the faith of both, had ceased to mention either, or to make quotations, as had so constantly been done, from their sacred books. After long neglect and silence, the Jewish and Christian tribes of the peninsula are noticed now, only to be condemned to perpetual vassalage:—

Jews and Christians to be made tributary.

Fight against those . . . who have received the Scriptures until they pay tribute with the hand, and are humbled. The Jews say that Ezra is the son of God, and the Christians that the Messiah is the Son of God. . . God destroy them! How they have devised lying vanities! They take their Priests and their Monks for lords besides God, and likewise the Messiah, son of Mary. Yet they were not bidden but to worship the One God alone. . . O ye Faithful! verily many of the Priests

Sura ix.

and Monks devour the substance of men in vanity, and obstruct the way of God. They that treasure up gold and silver, and spend it not in the ways of the Lord, announce unto them a grievous punishment; on the day when their gold and silver shall be heated in the fire of hell, and their foreheads, and their sides, and their backs shall be seared therewith, while it is said unto them, This is that which ye have treasured up for yourselves, wherefore taste ye of the same.

Judaism and Christianity contemptuously cast aside.

Thus with threats of abasement and cruel words, Mahomet parted with those to whose teaching he owed so much. Having reached the pinnacle of his ambition, he cast aside the ladder by which he had climbed to it. Yet even here a distinction is observable between their treatment and that of the heathen. These are not tolerated even on submission. Failing to embrace Islam, idolaters must be warred with to the bitter end. But Jews and Christians are permitted to continue such. They are, indeed, to be warred against; but on submission and "payment of tribute with their hand" they are to be maintained, though humbled and abased, in the undisturbed profession of their faith.[1]

[1] It is important to note, however, that the passage quoted is part of "the Discharge," and, like it, immediately applicable, in its original intention, only to the peoples of Arabia. But after Islam had burst the borders of the peninsula, it was held by the followers of the prophet to be of universal application. Consequently, all over the world, idolaters must be rooted out, while Jews and Christians are to be tolerated on becoming tributary.

CHAPTER XXXIV.

EMBASSIES TO MEDINA. A.D. 630, 631. A.H. IX., X.
ÆTAT. 62, 63.

Stream of embassies. A.H. IX., X.

THE life of Mahomet was drawing towards a close, and so also was the Mission he had set before himself. The proof was seen in the continuous and submissive embassies which from every side of the peninsula streamed ceaselessly towards Medina.

Supremacy secured by conquest of Mecca.

The conquest of Mecca and lordship over its Temple, paved the way for the assertion of a paramount authority over all Arabia. No such pretension, indeed, had ever been put forth by the Coreish as the guardians of the Káaba. Nevertheless, their jurisdiction was acknowledged not merely over the Holy places and the Pilgrimage, but also in respect of certain other matters, secular as well as spiritual, which affected the whole Arab race, such as the intercalation of the calendar, and regulation of the sacred months during which war was unlawful. Moreover, Mahomet had so deftly riveted the secular and the spiritual together, that whosoever acknowledged the one must needs equally acknowledge the other, and so yield an implicit obedience "to the Lord and His

P 2

prophet" in all things belonging to the State equally with those belonging to the Church. In recognition of the Divine right thus claimed, Mahomet, shortly after the taking of Mecca, demanded from all tribes tendering their adhesion to his faith, the prescribed tithe, being a tenth of all the increase. Messengers were sent in every quarter to assess the tithe and bring it to Medina. With few and unimportant exceptions they accomplished their errand peaceably, which is the more remarkable as the Bedouins are notorious for impatience of taxation in any shape.

Deputations from all parts of Arabia

The submission of Tâyif, and the fall of its famous idol, enhanced the fame of Mahomet far and near. The Ninth year of the Hegira is styled "the Year of Deputations," in virtue of the great number of embassies that presented themselves in it from distant quarters, as well as in the following year. The princes of Omân, Bahrein, Yemen, and Yemâma, either by letter or embassy, tendered allegiance; chiefs of such tribes as the kingly race of Kinda from Hadhramant, in the south, and the son of the famous Hâtim Tay, chief of the Beni Tay in the north, appeared in person; while warriors, poets, orators—men of renown from every part of Arabia—crowded to the simple court of Medina. On the other hand, legates were sent by Mahomet to the various provinces, and fixed at the seats of government as the resident Plenipotentiaries of the prophet; and Missionaries, or "Readers," followed in their steps to instruct the people in the Coran and the requirements of Islam. In the more remote parts, as Omân, the tithe was left in the hands of the local Ruler, for distribution among the poor of the country. Some of the embassies appeared at Medina with a pomp and following that contrasted strangely with the severe simplicity of Mahomet's life. Become now a powerful prince, he still maintained (save in the matter of wives and concubines) the frugal and unpretending habits of his earlier days.

Treaties with Christian tribes.

Some of the embassies came from Christian tribes. These were treated courteously. Some renounced their faith, tempted by the immunities of Islam. To one of these the prophet gave a vessel of water taken from his own ablutions, and bade them, after dismantling their church, to sprinkle the site with this water, and rear thereon a mosque. Another tribe was allowed to continue the profession of Christianity, but forbidden to baptize their children. The Christians of Najrân early tendered their submission, and were graciously received. The embassy was headed by the chief of the noble Kinda tribe and their bishop. On reaching Medina they entered the Great Mosque and prayed therein, turning towards the east. Then Mahomet recited to them passages from the Coran, and there followed an earnest disputation. At last he said, "If ye deny that which I say unto you, come, let us take an oath, laying the curse of God upon him that lieth." They declined. "We will not curse with thee," they said, "but we will give thee what thou demandest of us, and enter into treaty with thee." This was agreed to, and a rescript granted which guaranteed them in the undisturbed enjoyment of their Christian privileges, on a tribute of two thousand suits of raiment. And so they continued throughout the troublous times that followed the prophet's death, until Omar, minded to banish all other religions but Islam from the peninsula, expatriated them, and also the Jews of Kheibar, and settled them in the north.

The discussion with this embassy turned upon the Divinity of our Saviour, and is referred to in a passage of the Coran so curious that the reader may wish to see it:—

> Verily the analogy of Jesus is, with God, as that of Adam. The Lord created him from the dust, then said unto him, BE, and he was. Whosoever shall dispute with thee herein, say, *Come, let us call over the names of our Sons and your Sons, of our Wives and your Wives, of our own selves and your own selves; then let us curse one the other, and lay the curse of God on them that lie.* SAY, O ye People of the Book! come unto a just judgment between us and you, namely, that we shall not worship aught but the Lord, nor associate any other with Him.

Sura iii.

It was a strange method to propose for settling the question, and we have no reason to be ashamed of the Christian embassy for declining to enter upon such questionable ground. But we may, at the same time, accept the incident as significant of Mahomet's earnestness, and his conviction of the spiritual illumination which he believed to guide him.

Expeditions against Najrân and Yemen, A.D. 631. A.H. X.

The heathen tribes inhabiting Najrân embraced Islam at the summons of Khâlid, who was sent in the Tenth year of the Hegira to reduce them. Another expedition towards the close of the same year was undertaken by Aly, who proceeded with a squadron of three hundred horse against certain refractory tribes in Yemen. After a successful campaign he rejoined Mahomet on his Farewell Pilgrimage at Mecca.

MOUNT ARAFAT AT THE TIME OF THE PILGRIMAGE.

CHAPTER XXXV.

FAREWELL PILGRIMAGE. MARCH 632 A.D. A.H. X. ÆTAT. 63.

THE month of pilgrimage was again at hand. No idol would now offend the eye, nor any pagan by his presence pollute the Temple and the Holy places sacred to its worship. Mahomet might now without offence perform the sacred rites, and he prepared to do so. It is called the *Farewell Pilgrimage*, because on this occasion, as it were, he took his final leave of Mecca. He had not since the Flight gone up to the Greater Pilgrimage. This, therefore, was the only time when, as Ruler of the land, he observed its various ceremonies; and the precedent set by him on this occasion has ever since been followed to the most minute detail.

Annual pilgrimage, March 632 A.D. A.H. X.

Accompanied by vast multitudes, and by all his wives, Mahomet set out from Medina in time to take the journey leisurely. A hundred camels, marked by his own hand for sacrifice, were led in solemn order. Mosques had already sprung up along the road in the various halting-places, and at these Mahomet led the devotions of the thronging multitude. He halted an easy march from Mecca, and next morning, having bathed, he entered the city,

Mahomet sets out: end of Dzul Cada. A.H. X.

mounted on Al Caswa. As he approached the Káaba he raised his hands to heaven and invoked a blessing on the Holy place. Still mounted, he performed the preliminary rites of circumambulation of the Temple, and of going seven times to and fro between the eminences of Safa and Marwa. Then he retired to rest in a tent which had been pitched for him in the valley.

On the day preceding the first great day of Pilgrimage, Mahomet preached after the midday prayers to the multitudes assembled to make the seven circuits of the Káaba and drink of the well Zem-zem. Next day, followed by myriads of devotees, he set out for Mina, distant about six miles up the valley, performed there the customary prayers, and slept in a tent. At sunrise he passed onwards to Arafât. This is a small conical hill, a couple of hundred feet in height, about six miles further up the same valley, which here widens out into a plain hemmed in by granite peaks. Ascending the summit of this little isolated hill, the prophet stood there erect upon his camel, and declared the valley sacred, as the proper limit of the pilgrim tour. Then bowing low in prayer, he recited certain passages, ending with the Divine behest, "*This day have I perfected your religion unto you, and appointed for you Islam to be your faith.*"

Performs the pilgrimage to Arafât, 8th and 9th Dzul Hijj.

Sura v.

The day was passed in the ceremonies of Arafât, while the innumerable multitude of pilgrims spread out, shouting their *Labbeik,* in the plain below. At sunset Mahomet quitted the sacred mount on his way back, and by the bright moonlight returned half-way to Mina, sleeping at Mozdalifa. Next morning, before daylight, he sent the women and little

Sleeps at Mozdalifa, 9th Zul Hijj.

CASTING STONES IN THE DEFILE OF MINA.

ones ahead, lest the crowds hurrying along from Arafât should jostle them. As they went he touched one and another on the shoulder, saying, "My children, have a care that ye throw not the stones at the knoll of Acaba until the sun arise,"—an ancient rite in memory, they say, of Abraham, who cast stones at projecting eminences of the narrow Mina valley to drive the devil thence.

And completes the pilgrimage at Mina, 10th Dzul Hijj.

At dawn he arose to perform the matin prayer. Then, mounted on his camel, he resumed the march from Mozdalifa under a heavy shower of rain, shouting as he went the pilgrim cry—

> Labbeik, O Lord! Labbeik, Labbeik!
> There is no other God but Thee, Labbeik!
> Praise, blessing, and dominion be to Thee, Labbeik!
> No one therein may share with Thee, Labbeik!

He ceased not uttering these ejaculations till he entered the valley of Mina, and there cast stones at the "Devil's Corner." Then he slew the victims, and ended the ceremonies of pilgrimage by shaving his head and paring his nails. The *ihrâm*, or scanty pilgrim garb, was now exchanged for ordinary clothes, perfumes were burned, and the flesh of the sacrifices was distributed for food. Upon this, Aly, riding the prophet's mule, made proclamation throughout the concourse that, pilgrimage being over, it was now the time for eating and enjoyment. Mahomet spent three days at Mina, and every evening repeated the ceremony of casting stones at the customary spots.

Farewell discourse, 11th Dzul Hijj.

On the second of these days, Mahomet mounted his camel, and from the widening centre of the Mina valley addressed the vast assembly in words which the people felt, and probably he felt himself, to be his farewell to them. He enjoined the sacredness of life and property, and of inheritance; and then, as to the relations of the family, proceeded thus:—

O people! ye have rights demandable of your Wives, and your Wives have rights demandable of you. On them it is incumbent not to violate their conjugal duty, nor to commit any act of impropriety; which things if they do, ye have authority to shut them up in separate apartments, and to beat them with stripes, yet not severely. But if they refrain therefrom, clothe and feed them suitably. Treat well your women, for they are as your captives, and ye have made their persons lawful unto you by the words of God.

And your Slaves! See that ye feed them with such food as ye eat yourselves, and clothe them with the stuff ye wear. And if they commit a fault, then sell them, for they are servants of the Lord, and are not to be tormented.

Next he dwelt on the equality of believers. "Ye are one brotherhood," he said; and to give his words the greater emphasis, he placed the forefinger of one hand as an emblem of evenness on the forefinger of the other. Intercalation of the Calendar he abolished, declaring it an unhallowed innovation on the Divine arrangement of the months; and announced, "Now on this very day hath time performed its cycle, and come round to the self-same era as that on which God created the heavens and the earth." Then, having bidden them beware of the machinations of Satan even in things indifferent, he ended thus: "Verily I have fulfilled my mission. I have left amongst you a plain command, to wit, the Book of God and manifest ordinances, of which if ye take fast hold, ye shall never go astray." He stopped, and looking upwards, cried, "O Lord, I have delivered my message and discharged my Ministry!" The people shouted, "Yea, verily thou hast." Once more the prophet added, "Bear witness

Parting words.

thereunto, O Lord, I beseech Thee!" and with these words he dismissed the great assembly.

Next day the concourse broke up. Returning to Mecca, Mahomet once again made the seven circuits of the Káaba. Repairing to the well Zem-zem hard by, he called for a pitcher of the water, and having drunk from it, and rinsed his mouth in the same, commanded the contents to be thrown back into the well. Then taking off his shoes, he ascended the doorway of the Káaba, and having entered the sacred chamber prayed therein. The ceremonies ended, he departed to his tent. On the way, fatigued and thirsty, he stopped at the door of one who kept date-water for the pilgrims to drink, and quenched his thirst. He continued at Mecca three days, and then took his journey back to Medina.

Further ceremonies at Mecca.

CHAPTER XXXVI.

THREE PRETENDERS. A.D. 632. A.H. XI.

THE Eleventh year of Mahomet's residence at Medina opened peacefully. Already the greater part of the peninsula acknowledged his authority. The loose autonomy of the Arab tribes made it easy for Mahomet to assert his suzerainty without interfering in their internal affairs. In the more distant provinces, also, the prerogative was vague, and as yet put to no sufficient test. Still, there was, almost everywhere, the outward form of submission to all that had been demanded. The days of the prophet were now chiefly occupied in the reception of embassies, the issue of rescripts to his various delegates scattered over the land, and the consolidation of his power, both secular and spiritual.

A.H. XI. opens peacefully.

We must not, however, omit briefly to notice the rise of three Pretenders who questioned his authority. Strange to say, these laid claim themselves to the same prophetic office; but the standing and influence to which during his lifetime they attained, were not such as to cause him any great uneasiness. One was Toleiha, chief of the Beni Asad,

Three Pretenders.

in Nejd; and another Moseilama, ruler of Yemâma, in the centre of Arabia. Neither of them gave any serious trouble till after the prophet's death. Moseilama sent an arrogant despatch to Medina, demanding that Mahomet should "divide the land with him." When the letter was read out, the prophet turned to the two envoys who ventured to urge their master's claim, saying, "By the Lord, if it were not that ambassadors are sacred, I would have beheaded both of you." Then he sent them away with the haughty answer: "Thine epistle with its lies and fabrications against the Lord hath been read to me. Verily the earth is the Lord's, and He causeth such of His servants as He pleaseth to inherit the same. Peace be to him that followeth the true direction!" The battle of Yemâma, with its *Garden of Death*, was a perilous day for Islam, but the story belongs to the Caliphate of the prophet's Successor. Toleiha also, after the prophet's death, withstood the arms of Abu Bekr, but he was defeated by Khâlid, and having tendered his submission, fought bravely with his tribe in the battles of Islam.

Toleiha and Moseilama.

Aswad, the "Veiled Prophet" of Yemen, was the third Pretender. Towards the end of the Tenth year of the Hegira, he raised the standard of rebellion, and drove out the officers of Mahomet. Falling upon Sanaâ, he slew the governor, took his widow to wife, and established himself in independent authority. The insurrection spread into Najrân and the surrounding districts. Mahomet, imperfectly informed of the extent of the rising, contented himself with instructing his adherents to compass the death of the Usurper, or to attack him if possible in force. Fortunately for Islam, Aswad, in the pride of conquest, had already begun to

Aswad in Yemen.

slight the commanders to whose bravery he owed his success. The agents of Mahomet, through these, and in league with the tyrant's wife, plotted his assassination. He was slain about the very time of Mahomet's death; and peace would immediately have been restored, had not the tidings of that event,—the death, namely, of the prophet,—again thrown the province into confusion. The campaign that ensued belongs to the reign of Abu Bekr.

CHAPTER XXXVII.

SICKNESS AND DEATH OF MAHOMET. JUNE 632 A.D. A.H. XI. ÆTAT. 63.

Preparations for campaign on Syrian border, May 632 A.D. Safar, A.H. IX.

ABOUT two months after his return from the Farewell Pilgrimage, Mahomet gave orders for an expedition to the Syrian frontier. The reverse at Mûta had not yet been sufficiently avenged. Moreover, the Christian and pagan tribes on the border, and beyond it, were of Arabian lineage, and as such, equally with the dwellers in the peninsula, amenable to the faith of Islam and the authority of its Founder. It was necessary to enforce the allegiance of the wavering, and strike terror into the hearts of the recalcitrant. Such were the objects of the expedition; and to mark its immediate purpose, the command was given to Osâma, son of Zeid, with these words: "March to the place where thy father was slain, and destroy it utterly. Lo, therefore have I made thee Commander of this army. Fall suddenly upon the land at early morn, and let the fire devour it utterly. Hasten thy steps, so that thine onset precede the tidings of thee. But withal take guides, and send before thee scouts and spies." The following day Mahomet was prostrated with fever, but on the third day he so far recovered as to bind with his own hand the banner for the army and present it to Osâma. He urged forward the levy with all despatch, and gave command that the camp should be formed on the plain at Jorf.

Mahomet falls sick, May 27th, 632 A.D. 1st Rabi I., A.H. XI.

It was the beginning of the third month of the Eleventh year of the Hegira that Mahomet fell sick. He never but once had suffered from any serious illness. A few years previously he was seized with an attack which caused him to pine away and even neglect his wives. The cause, we are told, was certain incantations of the Jews over knots tied with hair taken from his head. The spell was discovered and broken, and soon after he recovered. The poisoned shoulder of mutton of which he partook at Kheibar was followed by effects more potent and more lasting. To it Mahomet ascribed an excruciating pain which periodically seized his back, and of which he now complained. When attacked by his last illness, he did not at once succumb, but maintained the custom of visiting his wives' apartments in succession. Once in the still of night he rose, restless, and followed only by a servant, repaired to the burial-ground in the outskirts of the city, where he waited long, absorbed in meditation. Then, apostrophizing the dead, he prayed thus aloud: "Verily ye, and I also, have obtained that which the Lord did promise us. Blessed are ye! Your lot is better than the lot of them that are left behind. Lord, have mercy on the men that lie buried here!" With these words he turned and departed to his house. In the morning, as he was passing by the chamber of Ayesha, who too was ailing, he heard her moan, and thus addressed her;—"Nay, Ayesha, it is I who should

Visits the burial-ground by night.

cry, 'My head, my head!'" Then, in a tenderer strain, (yet haply with a touch of plaintive humour,) "But wouldest not thou desire to be taken first, while I am yet alive, so that I might pray over thee, and, wrapping thee in thy winding-sheet, myself commit thee to the grave?" "That happen to another, and not to me," said Ayesha, adding archly,—"Ah! that, I see, is what thou wishest for! Truly, I can see thee, when all was over, returning straightway hither, and sporting with a new wife in my chamber here!" He smiled, but was too ill for a rejoinder in the same strain. And so, complaining again sadly of his head, he passed on to the apartment of Meimûna, whose day it was. The fever returning violently upon him, he called his wives together and said, "Ye see that I am very sick. I am not able to visit you in turn. If it be pleasing unto you, I will remain in the house of Ayesha." They agreed. And so, his head bound round with a napkin, and his clothes wrapped loosely about him, he walked, supported by Aly and Abbâs, to the apartment of Ayesha. Hardly yet twenty years of age, she tended with affection and solicitude the death-bed of her aged husband.

Retires to Ayesha's apartment.

Mahomet continued for some days to lead, though feebly, the public prayers. He had been ill about a week, when, perceiving the sickness gain ground, with occasional fits of swooning, he resolved on an effort to address the people, whose murmurs at the youth of Osâma as commander of the Syrian expedition, had reached his ears. Refreshed by seven skins of water poured over him, with his head bandaged and skirts girt loosely round (for it was summer), he went forth at the time of prayer into the court of the Mosque, and, when the service was over,

Chides the people for discontent at Osâma's command.

seated himself upon the pulpit. He reproved the people for their discontent, and expatiated on the merits of Osâma;—"A man," he said, "beloved of me, even as his father was. Wherefore do ye treat him well, for he is amongst the best of you." After a pause he added enigmatically, "Verily the Lord hath offered to one of His servants the choice betwixt this present life and that which is nigh unto Himself, and the servant hath chosen that which is nigh unto his Lord." Abu Bekr, quick to catch his meaning, burst into tears. Mahomet bade him not to weep, and immediately gave a touching proof of his special affection. "Now," said he, "let every door that leadeth into the Mosque be closed, saving only that which openeth from the habitation of Abu Bekr." Thus the place was hushed, as became the precincts of death; frequented only by worshippers and by whispering inquirers after the prophet's health.

Abu Bekr leads the prayers while Mahomet is laid aside.

The strain of this address aggravated the sickness of Mahomet. On the following day he attempted to rise at the time of prayer, but felt his strength give way. Accordingly, he gave command that Abu Bekr should lead the service in his stead. Having done so, he fell back in a swoon. Soon recovering, he was angry to find that the order had not been carried out. Ayesha began to expostulate, when he exclaimed impatiently, "Truly ye are every one of you like the foolish women of Joseph.[1] Give command forthwith!" It was given. And so Abu Bekr conducted the public prayers during the few remaining days of the prophet's life. Mahomet was now too weak to attend to

[1] See Sura xii. 32; referring to the legend that the women of Egypt fell to cutting their hands with knives, out of admiration of Joseph's beauty.

any business. But the Syrian expedition weighed upon his mind, and he kept saying from time to time, "Send quickly off the army of Osâma." He also inquired about the embassies daily arriving at Medina, and enjoined their hospitable entertainment.

The fever had now lasted nearly a fortnight, when on the night of Saturday, the eleventh day of the month, the fever came upon him in great violence. Racked and restless, he tossed upon his bed. During an alarming paroxysm Omm Salma screamed. "Hush!" said Mahomet, "no one crieth so, saving the unbeliever." At another time, to keep him quiet, Ayesha said, "Had one of us moaned thus, surely thou wouldest have found fault." "True," he answered, "but I burn with the heat of any two of you together." "Then," exclaimed a third, "thou shalt surely have the double reward." "Yea," rejoined Mahomet; "for there is not upon earth a believer sore afflicted, but the Lord causeth his sins to fall off from him, even as fall the leaves from off the trees in autumn." Omar having placed his hand upon the sufferer's head, suddenly withdrew it. "O prophet," he said, "how fierce the fever is upon thee!" "Yea, verily," he replied; "but during the night I have been repeating, in praise of the Lord, seventy Suras." "Rather," answered Omar, "why not take thy rest; for hath not the Lord said that all thy sins are forgiven thee, the former and the latter?" "Not so," said Mahomet; "for wherefore should I not yet be a faithful servant unto Him?"

Accession of fever, Saturday, 6th June, 11th Rabi I.

On Sunday he lay all through the day in weakness, with occasional delirium. Osâma, visiting him from the army, stooped down and kissed

Sunday, June 7th, 12th Rabi I. Delirium.

his face; but there was no audible response. Mahomet only raised his hands in the attitude of blessing, and laid them on the young commander's head, who then returned to his camp. During a swoon his wives administered some physic to him. Reviving, he asked what they had been doing to him. On being told, he exclaimed, "Out upon you! What is this but a physic for the pleurisy, which ye have learned in Abyssinia,—an evil disease is that, which the Lord will not let attack me. Now shall ye all of you in this chamber partake of the same, even as ye have physicked me, save only Abbâs, my uncle." So the women arose and poured the physic, in presence of the dying prophet, into each other's mouths.

In delirium curses Jews and Christians.

After this strange scene, the conversation turned upon the cathedral of Mâria, in Abyssinia. Two of his wives spoke of the wonderful pictures and decorations which when in exile they had seen upon its walls. Overhearing it, Mahomet was displeased, and said, "These are the men that build churches over their saints' tombs, and then garnish them with pictures,—the worst part are they of all creation." Then casting off the bed-clothes, probably in delirium, he said, "The Lord destroy the Jews and Christians! Let His anger kindle against such as turn their prophets' tombs into places of worship! Lord, let not my tomb ever be the object of worship. Let there be but one faith through all Arabia." About this time, recognizing Omar, he called out, "Fetch me hither pen and ink, that I may make a writing for you that shall keep you from straying into error for ever."[1] Omar said, "He wandereth in his mind." But the women answered,

Calls for writing materials.

[1] The words read as if in his delirium he wanted to write with his own hand, but probably he thought only to dictate a

"Come, let us ask him, and see whether he wandereth or not." So they asked him concerning that which he spoke of, but he had no longer any thought of it. "Leave me thus alone," he said; "my present state is better than that which ye call me to." Then he desired Ayesha to distribute six golden pieces he had in keeping, as alms, and said, "Now I am at peace. Verily, it would not have become me to meet my Lord, and this gold in my possession."

Monday morning, 8th June, 13th Rabí I. Mahomet enters Mosque.

All Sunday night the fever lay heavy upon Mahomet. They overheard him praying, "O my soul, why seek thy refuge elsewhere than in thy Lord alone?" The morning brought relief, and there was some return of strength. The Mosque was crowded with anxious worshippers. Abu Bekr, standing in the place of the prophet in front of the assembly, led the prayers. He had ended the first prostration, and begun the second, when the curtain of Ayesha's door slowly moved aside, and Mahomet entered the court. He whispered in the ear of the attendant on whom he leaned, "The Lord hath now verily granted me refreshment in prayer," and he looked around upon the worshippers with a gladsome smile. Pausing thus for a moment, and supported as before, he crept softly to the front, the people opening out before him. Abu Bekr heard the rustle, and guessing the cause (for he never turned at prayer), stepped back to vacate the leader's place. But Mahomet motioned to him to go on, and sat down on the ground for the rest of the service.

---

writing; for it is extremely doubtful whether Mahomet could write; certainly we do not ever read of his writing. He was fond moreover of the title of the "illiterate" prophet, as showing how dependent he was on the inspiration from heaven.

When it was ended, Abu Bekr entered into conversation with him. He rejoiced at his convalescence, and begged permission to visit his wife who lived in the upper suburb, and whose turn it was. Mahomet gave him leave, and he went.

Mahomet then sat down for a little in the court of the Mosque by Ayesha's door, and spoke to the people who crowded round him. He bade Osâma go forward with his army. Then turning to the women about him, he said, "Oh, Fâtima my daughter, and thou Safia my aunt, work ye out that which shall win you acceptance with the Lord, for I verily have not power to save you in any wise." Having said this, he was helped back into the chamber of Ayesha.

Mahomet speaks to the people.

It was but the flicker of an expiring taper. Exhausted, he lay down upon the bed, a mattress stretched upon the floor. Ayesha, seeing him very low and weak, raised his head from the pillow, as she sat by him on the ground, and placed it on her bosom. One entered at the moment with a green tooth-pick in his hand. Seeing his eye rest upon it, and knowing it to be just such as he liked, Ayesha took and chewed it a little to soften it, and then placed it in his hand. The thing pleased him, and rubbing with it his teeth for a moment with his ordinary vigour, he put the tooth-pick down again. His strength now rapidly sank. He called for a pitcher of water, and wetting his face from it, prayed, "O Lord, I beseech Thee, assist me in the agonies of death. Come close, O Gabriel, to me!"

Exhausted, he retires to Ayesha's chamber,

He now began to blow upon himself, ejaculating all the while petitions which he was used to repeat in the sick room.[1] When from weakness he ceased, Ayesha took up the task. Then she took his hand and rubbed it (as he himself used to do with the sick), still reciting the prayers. But even this he could not bear, saying, "Take thy hand from off me; it cannot help me now." After a little, in a whisper, "Lord, grant me pardon." Then at intervals, "Eternity in paradise!" "Pardon!" "The blessed Companionship on high!" He stretched himself gently; his head grew heavy on the breast of Ayesha; the prophet of Arabia was no more.

And dies in the arms of Ayesha,

Softly removing his head from her bosom, Ayesha replaced it on the pillow. Then she rose and joined the other women, who were beating their faces with loud lamentation. It was a little after midday. But a moment, as it were, ago, Mahomet had entered the Mosque, cheerful, and to appearance convalescent. He lay now cold in death.

Who replaces his head upon the pillow.

[1] Such as, "Remove the evil, O Lord of mankind! Heal, O Thou best of Physicians! There is not any cure but Thine, for it leaveth nought of the disease behind."

CHAPTER XXXVIII.

BURIAL. 8TH AND 9TH JUNE, A.D. 632.

Abu Bekr visits the chamber of death.

WHEN he heard the startling news, Abu Bekr hastened back to the Mosque. There he found Omar addressing the crowd in an excited frame. "The prophet was but in a trance," he said, "and would revive again, to root out all the hypocrites from off the land." Not heeding him, Abu Bekr passed on to Ayesha's door. He drew aside the curtain, entered, and stooping down kissed the face of his departed friend. "Sweet wast thou in life," he said, "and sweet thou art in death, dearer than father and mother to me! Yes, thou art dead, and" (referring to Omar's wild words without) "thou art too precious for the Lord to give thee to drink the bitter cup of death a second time." He covered over the face again, and withdrew. Omar was still haranguing the people. Abu Bekr sought to silence him; but it was not till he had quoted some verses from the Coran signifying the mortality of Mahomet as of other prophets before him, that the truth forced itself on the mind of Omar.

Just then one came running to say that the men of the city were assembled to choose an Ameer (or ruler) from amongst themselves. Followed by Omar, Abu Bekr hastened to the conclave just in time to interpose. Words ran high between them. They would divide the command. "An Ameer from us," they cried, "and an Ameer from you." "Never!" said Abu Bekr; "it cannot be. *We* are the Ameers. None but the Coreish will Arabia obey." The words began to tell, and Omar, seeing his opportunity, seized the hand of Abu Bekr and cried, "Did not the prophet himself appoint thee to lead the prayers? Thou art our master, whom the prophet loved the best of all, and (striking his hand) to thee we pledge allegiance." The rest followed Omar's example, recognizing him thus as the Caliph,[1] or Successor of the prophet.

Abu Bekr chosen Caliph or successor.

During the night the body was washed and laid out by Aly, Osâma, and others in Ayesha's apartment, and there also, just beneath the spot where he had breathed his last, the grave was dug. On the morrow, people thronged the chamber. They came in by companies at the door opening from the court of the Mosque, and after gazing at the remains and praying over them, passed out on the opposite side. The place was crowded when Abu Bekr and Omar entered together, and, standing before the body, prayed thus: "Peace be on thee, O prophet of the Lord, and His mercy and blessing! We bear witness that Thy prophet hath delivered the message revealed unto him; hath fought in the ways of the Lord, until that the Lord brought forth His religion unto victory; hath drawn us unto Himself, and been kind and tender-hearted to

The body lies in state.

[1] In the original, *Khaleefa*.

all believers, and hath not sought any recompense for delivering unto us the faith." The people answered *Amen, Amen!* After the men, the women followed in companies, and then even the children crowded round the bier for a last look at their prophet's face.

The court was filled with mourners when Abu Bekr, ascending the pulpit, was saluted Caliph by acclamation. His words were simple but firm. "Ye people," he said, "verily I am now your chief, albeit I am not the best amongst you. If I do well, support me; if ill, then set me right." He promised to rule justly, and without respect of persons, and concluded thus: "Leave not off to fight in the ways of the Lord; for whoso leaveth off to fight, him shall the Lord abase. Obey me whereinsoever I obey the Lord and His prophet; wherein I disobey, in that obey me not. Now arise to prayer, and the Lord be with you!" On that the assembly rose up to prayer, and Abu Bekr for the first time as Caliph filled his master's place.

Inaugural speech of Abu Bekr.

In the evening the final rites were paid to the remains of Mahomet. His red mantle was spread at the bottom of the grave; then the body was lowered into its last resting-place by the same loving hands that had laid it out. The vault was built over with bricks and the grave made level with the floor.

Burial.

In process of time Abu Bekr, and some years after Omar, who succeeded him as Caliph, were laid side by side with the prophet. Ayesha, till her death, continued to live on in the adjoining chamber.

Abu Bekr and Omar buried by him.

The Great Mosque, with the grave of Mahomet, is still

visited with the profoundest reverence by his followers, generally after they have made the pilgrimage to Mecca. The place has grown to great magnificence, but the worship celebrated (there as in Islam everywhere) is that same simple form of prayer which Mahomet inaugurated on the self-same spot thirteen centuries ago.

His grave a place of pilgrimage.

And so is it with the whole fabric of Islam; it remains precisely as the prophet left it, neither taken from nor added to,—his work alone. As the faith issued from the lips of Mahomet or was embodied in his daily life, even so it lived, and still lives the religion of a hundred and seventy-three millions of our race. "This day," as he said at the Farewell Pilgrimage, "have I perfected your religion unto you;" and for weal or woe, thus perfect and complete, it has ever since remained.

Islam remains exactly as it was left by Mahomet.

APPENDIX.

I.

THE CORAN AND TRADITION.

The Coran, and Tradition.

A SHORT narrative of the Coran and of Tradition may be acceptable to the reader, both as explaining the materials from which this biography has been drawn (for the student has no other source to draw from than native authority), and also as showing the ground on which Islam itself stands.

The Coran, as "collected" by Zeid, A.D. 633. A.H. XII.

The CORAN. At the death of Mahomet, the various Suras and fragments of his "Revelation" were still loose and scattered in the hands of the people. No attempt had been made as yet to gather them into one collection. But a great number of the chapters, in continuous form, whether written or committed to memory, were used as occasion required both in the public and in the private devotions of the Moslems. The originals, probably of the more important passages, are said to have been kept in a chest by one of the prophet's wives; others were in possession of the scribes or secretaries who first took them down; others again, and these chiefly the earlier deliverances, were mere scraps and fragments here and there and anywhere. It was not till the battle of Yemâma, the year after Mahomet's death, that Omar suggested to the Caliph Abu Bekr the design of having the whole Coran written out continuously, while it was yet fresh in the memory of believers. "I fear," he said, "lest slaughter should again wax hot among the Reciters[1] of the Coran in other fields of battle, and that much of the sacred text may be lost. Now, therefore, I advise that thou give command for its collection." The commission was given to Zeid, who had been the chief secretary of the prophet. He at once set about the task of gathering together not only the completed passages and Suras, but also detached fragments and fugitive verses from every quarter, and the whole he recorded in one consecutive roll. His object was that no word or syllable which had dropped in the way of "inspiration" from the lips of Mahomet should be lost, but should find its place in this collection. So we are told that Zeid sought out not only what was written in rolls, but also such remains as were inscribed "on palm leaves, on shreds of leather and parchment, on shoulder-blades and tablets of stone, and in the breasts of men." These were arranged and rudely dove-tailed together without much regard to chronology, but with some respect to the subject and context. Thus by his labours the confused materials assumed the form in which we now find them. And hence it is that the Coran in so many parts bears traces of haphazard collection and fortuitous arrangement; and of the consequent obscurity and incoherence which weary and perplex the reader.

In the reign of Othmân, some fifteen years later, the copies used in distant lands were found to vary so much from one another, that the Caliph caused a collation of the same, and

[1] The *Reciters of the Coran* are those who had committed it to memory. It was (and still is) a religious merit to do so. Many had the text, more or less complete, by heart, and were in the habit of thus, quite independently of any manuscript, reciting it.

therefrom a recension to be made, and an authoritative text laid down. Exemplars of the standard version were deposited in the chief cities, and all the former copies were called in and burned. Uniformity has ever since been enforced by law; and so in the hundreds and thousands of copies throughout the Moslem world, there is but one Coran, with no differences of any kind, and with hardly the approach even to a various reading.

Othmân's recension.

But if the text be one, there are plentiful discrepancies of meaning in various passages showing the changes which took place in the author's mind. Where these amount to irreconcilable contradictions, theologians hold that the passage last revealed cancels the first. But they are not always agreed which that last may be. The several chapters are headed "Meccan" Suras or "Medina" Suras, according as in the order of time they were produced either in the one city or in the other. So great, however, is the confusion of the subject-matter, that many passages belonging clearly to Medina appear in Meccan Suras, and *vice versâ.* The unlearned reader is further puzzled by the relative order of the Suras themselves. There is here no respect of time whatever. The longer Suras, as a rule, come first, and the shorter last. Now, as in point of fact the later Suras were the longest, and the earlier the shortest, the natural order has as a rule been just inverted; and the student, instead of reading from the beginning to the end, would have a better idea of the chronological sequence of the several parts, if he read from the end to the beginning—from the last Sura backwards to the first.

Chronological confusion.

With all these defects, the Coran is held in the utmost possible veneration and regard by Moslems, as the divine and even "eternal" Book of God.

Decisive authority of Coran.

It has been so in every age and land and by almost every sect. Its word is absolute, whether in matters secular or spiritual, whether in Church or State. Its meaning may be variously interpreted, but its authority is unquestioned, and its judgment final.

After the Coran, and of a secondary character, comes TRADITION, that is, the teaching of Mahomet, whether by word of mouth or by act and precedent. Islam at its rise was severely theocratic. The whole life, civil and religious, hung upon the Law and the Prophet. At first the Coran, as embodying the former, sufficed for the simple wants of Arab society. But as the faith spread into other lands, some highly civilized, it soon became too scant for the sole rule of life. To amplify the canon, resort was had to the precedent of Mahomet himself. What did he say or do? or, What under the circumstances would he have said or done? His "Companions" are the authorities from whom the answers to these questions emanate. From them have descended a vast mass of traditions, each embodying some saying, or stating some habit or act of the prophet, all of which, according to their credibility, are used to supplement the Coran as a guide of faith and practice. But the authority of these traditions is of every shade, "weak," "probable," or "undisputed," according to the character of the chain of witnesses whose names from first to last are noted separately for each. Thousands and hundreds of thousands of such traditions were handed down, orally at first, but in process of time committed to writing. On these, in addition to the Coran, the Schools of theology and law have been built. Besides the four Schools called the *Orthodox*, there is the *Sheeah* sect (chiefly followed in Persia), who, disallowing the first three Caliphs as well as all "orthodox"

Tradition.

R 2

tradition, recognize only the succession of Aly, and the legitimacy of the prophet's line. The practice and tenets of the various sects differ widely. But all Moslems recognize the authority of Mahomet's precedent (if the tradition delivering it be credible) as binding, though always second to the Coran, for that is absolute and indefeasible.

Islam the work of Mahomet alone.

Thus Islam is the work of Mahomet, sole and alone. It was begun by him, and as he left it, so we find it now. Its only ground-work, and its final test, is his word and deed. "This day," as at the *Farewell Pilgrimage* he proclaimed from Mount Arafât, "have I (the Lord) perfected your Faith unto you, and fulfilled My mercy upon you, and appointed Islam for you to be your Religion."

II.

OBSERVANCES AND LAWS OF ISLAM.

Ritual. Rites and ceremonies.

Such being the canon, few words are needed to make the reader who has studied this volume understand what are the observances of Islam. As the day began with the prophet, so with his followers ever since, it opens with prayer,—the Muedzin, like Bilâl, arousing the sleepers far and near to their devotions. Five times a day, as the proper hour comes round, the ceremony is repeated, when the believer, whether in Mosque or at home or by the way, must prostrate himself in worship with his face toward the Holy house at Mecca. At mid-day on Friday there is a more general or Cathedral service, with a sermon, which should be attended by the community at large in the Mosque. Prayer must in every case of legal impurity, as with the Jews, be preceded by lustration. In the desert, where

Prayer.

there is no water, sand may be substituted for it. With the fast of Ramadhân (or Ramzân) the reader is already familiar; as well as with the Eed al Fitr, or festival of breaking the fast after the month is ended; for they are all observed just as the prophet commanded, or by his own act set the example. Pilgrimage to Mecca is obligatory on every Moslem having the means, at the least once in his lifetime. Those who stay at home are still in the habit of slaying their victims on the great day of sacrifice, as Mahomet did at Medina.[1] The tithe of the increase is rendered by all, to "purify" that which remains. Circumcision is not mentioned in the Coran, but, having been in vogue among the Arabs, is held to be incumbent on Mahometans when the child has reached the age of boyhood.

Fasting.

Pilgrimage.

The *Moharram*, observed with great pomp and display of grief over the Moslem world, on the tenth of that month, is not prescribed, like the other ordinances, by tradition or the Coran, since it is in commemoration of the fate of Hosein and his little party slain near Kûfa, forty years after the death of his grandfather, the prophet.

Moharram.

The central tenet of Islam is the Unity of God. The "association" of any other person with the Deity is the one mortal sin. Idolatry is to be rooted out, and images utterly abolished. There is no priesthood in Islam. Mahomet is the prophet through whom God has made known the last and perfect revelation of Himself. And the Faith is summed up in this short and decisive creed,—*There is no God but the Lord, and Mahomet is His prophet,*—the simple confession of which makes the convert

Doctrine.
Unity of the Deity.

[1] This is the festival which in Constantinople is called *Corban Beiram*, and in Egypt *Eed al Corbân*, "the day of sacrifice."—Lane's *Modern Egyptians*, II. p. 251.

a Mussulman. The theocratic element of the early Caliphate is preserved more or less in all Moslem lands. The Church and State are absolutely one, and as such the chief ruler presides at prayer. The authority of leading Doctors, as the Sheikh ul Islam, Moulas (learned Scholars), and Cazies or Judges, is recognized, but simply as exponents of the Divine law. That law cannot be changed, improved, or developed; it can only be made clear and interpreted.

Relation to Islam of preceding Revelations.

Before Mahomet were many prophets. Such were Noah, Abraham "the friend of God," David, Solomon, and so forth, through whom God made revelation of Himself from time to time. The last and greatest before Mahomet was Jesus the Messiah, born of a Virgin, "the Word of God and a Spirit from Him." He wrought miracles and revealed the gospel. The Jews intended to crucify Him, but failed, and He ascended into heaven. The Trinity and the Sonship and Divinity of Jesus are vehemently denounced, as well as the worship of His Mother. The books of the Old and New Testaments are recognized, especially in the earlier portions of the Coran, as authoritative and Divine; but theologians, finding that these do not correspond with their own Revelation, were early led to cut the knot by asserting that they had been corrupted—the context dislocated and the teaching altered,—at the hands of Jews and Christians.

Tenets.

With the most important tenets of Islam the reader is already familiar. Such are the special providence of the Deity, extending to the minutest concerns of daily life; the ministry of good angels; the hateful influence of the devil and fallen angels; the existence of a race intermediate between angels and men, called *Jinn* or Genii; the immortality of the soul; the resurrection of the body; the judgment of good and evil; heaven and hell. The teaching of Mahomet, taken mainly from the Jews, partly from the Christians, partly also from the Magians, was engrafted on the native worship and tradition of Arabia. We should mistake, however, if we ascribed to Mahomet any scheme of systematic theology. His creed was developed by the conditions and exigencies of the day. It was concrete, grew out of circumstance. While, therefore, we find him holding firmly and constantly by certain cardinal points, as the Unity and attributes of Deity, retribution of good and evil, &c., we shall not be surprised at the occasional appearance of change and inconsistency in others of his utterances. And hence it arose that when philosophers and divines began to elaborate from his teaching a system of ethics and theology, there was large room for variety of doctrine. For example, although Predestination pervades the Coran, and is pronounced sometimes in a painful and offensive way,[1] yet elsewhere there are deliverances of an opposite character, from which some schools have deduced the dogma of Free-will, and taught the same in its most absolute form. On the whole, however, a strong tincture of fatalism pervades the Moslem mind. Salvation is promised to all believers, but even for them the retribution is held of good and evil works. Hell, as an endless state, is reserved for unbelievers and polytheists. And so theologians have found an intermediate state of temporary punishment for believers whose evil works outweigh their good; that is to say, they hold a kind of purgatory, of which there is no distinct trace in the Coran itself. There are many points of doctrine and fine casuistry which have been fiercely contested by the different

[1] For example, in such verses as these:—"God misleadeth whom He pleaseth, and guideth aright whom He pleaseth." "If the Lord pleased, He had made all men of one faith, . . but unto this end hath He created them, for the word of the Lord shall be fulfilled, Verily I will fill hell altogether with Men and Genii."

schools, and by hosts even on the battle-field: as the Divine succession to the Caliphate, the creation of the Coran or its eternity, the perceptibility by the creature of the Creator, &c. But it is unnecessary to pursue the subject here.

Prohibitions. Of the negative precepts of the Coran, it is needful only to mention the prohibition of wine, a restriction rigorously observed in Moslem lands, excepting among some of the laxer sections of the upper classes. Games of chance and the taking of usury are also proscribed. Following the Jewish law, swine's flesh and blood, things strangled, that which dieth of itself, meats offered to idols, and animals over which in slaying them God's name has not been spoken, are all forbidden.

Relations of the sexes. It remains briefly to notice the relations established by the Coran between the sexes. Every Moslem is allowed four free wives, and he may at the same time legally cohabit with as many as he likes of the slave-girls which "his right hand may possess." The progeny of bondwomen by their masters is legitimate, and inherits equally with that of the free wives. The husband can at any time divorce his wife, without the assignment of any reason, at his simple pleasure. The wife has no corresponding privilege; she cannot be freed from her bondage, however galling, until the husband chooses to divorce her. Moreover, if he should repeat the words of divorce thrice, he cannot take her back until the unfortunate woman has been married to another husband, and after consummation been by him divorced.

Slavery. Slavery is recognized as a civil institution in the Coran. It is perpetuated not only by the bondage of the progeny of slaves, but also by the fresh accession of men, women, and children taken captive in Jehâd, or religious war. The obligation of fighting for the extension of Islam, however much it may have fallen into desuetude from the political and military decline of Moslem states, still survives; and under cover of it, raids even in the present day are carried on against the heathen tribes of Africa and Asia.[1] It is true that, apart from the horrors of war and the slave trade, slavery in Mahometan countries is mainly a domestic institution involving easy service. But not the less has it a demoralizing influence on society at large, and more especially in its bearing on servile concubinage does it defile the springs of purity and virtue.

With the Veil, as instituted by Mahomet, the reader is already sufficiently acquainted. Prescribed in the Coran, it is obligatory on all who acknowledge the authority of the Book. Taken in conjunction with the other restrictions there imposed on domestic life, it has led to the institution of the Harem and Zenâna,—that is, the private portion of the home in which women are, with more or less of stringency in various lands, secluded from the outer world. With polygamy, concubinage, and arbitrary divorce, some such restraint may be necessary to check the loose matrimonial standard which might otherwise undermine the decencies of social life. But the institution of the Veil has not the less chilled and checked all civilizing influences, and rendered rude and barbarous the Moslem world. It is impossible for a people who, contrary to nature, exclude from their outer life the whole female sex, materially to rise in the scale of civilization.

The Veil and the Harem.

And so it ever must remain as long as Islam endures. For the Veil, and the other sexual relations that make it necessary, are bound up together in the

Coran checks civilizing influences.

[1] As against the Siâhposh, or Kaffre tribes in the hill ranges to the north-west of India.

Coran, and from the Coran it is impossible for the loyal and consistent Moslem to turn aside. And herein lies the secret of the backwardness of Moslem lands, and their failure to keep pace with the civilized world in the march of moral and material progress.

III.

ISLAM AND CHRISTIANITY.

Islam and other religions.

Though it is not the purpose of this work to compare Islam with the other religions of the world, yet the estimate of its doctrines and practices would be incomplete without a review of how it stands in its relation towards them.

Islam and barbarous religions.

There can be no question but that, with its pure monotheism, and a code founded in the main on justice and humanity, Islam succeeds in raising to a higher level races sunk in idolatry and fetichism, like those of Central Africa, and that in some respects—notably in that of temperance—it materially improves the morality of such peoples. But, having raised them to a certain point, it leaves them there. Whether in things secular or spiritual, there is no advance. The defects of which I have been treating cling to the outer life; and as regards the inner life, there is, in the cold and formal round of Moslem ordinances, altogether wanting the genial and motive power of the Heavenly Father's love.

Code of Islam hard and fast.

When, again, we come to compare Islam with Christianity, and first in its secular aspect, one is immediately struck with the difference between the two in the virtue of adaptation to the wants and aspirations of humanity. Islam imposes a code, hard, fast, and imperative in every detail, which, however well it may have suited Arabia thirteen centuries ago, is quite unfitted for the varying requirements of other times and places. Yet it binds society hand and foot; there can be no onward, upward movement, nor even the attempt to rise.

The Christian code is altogether different. It lays down principles, and not details. If there be one exception,—that, namely, in respect of marriage and divorce,—it is expressly based on the laws of nature. "He," said Jesus, "which made them at the beginning, made them male and female; . . what, therefore, God hath joined together, let not man put asunder." The foundations of Christian morality are not less immutable than those of the Coran, but they are infinitely broader, and can be built on for all generations. Its laws are capable of being applied to the habits, thought, and institutions of all ages, and its doctrines harmonize with every upward step towards freedom, knowledge, and philanthropy; indeed, we may say, themselves contain the plastic force which brings these results about. In short, the distinction between the two creeds is, that while the aspirations of humanity have free play under the Gospel, in the swathing bands of the Coran they are altogether checked and stifled.

Christianity adaptive to the wants of humanity.

Two of the institutions of Islam which we have just been considering will illustrate this, namely, the Veil and Slavery. The Moslem lady must be shrouded from the eye of man for all time to come. The Gospel simply enjoins upon the sex that their conversation be discreet and chaste, and that "they adorn themselves in modest apparel, with shamefacedness and sobriety."[1] And

Illustrated by the Veil and Slavery.

[1] 1 Tim. ii. 9; Titus ii. 4, 5; 1 Peter iii. 3.

so while Mussulman society is debarred from the softening and ameliorating influences of the sex beyond the precincts of the Harem, the Christian lady can take her place side by side with man as his helpmeet, and the handmaid of mercy and benevolence. So it is also with Slavery. In Islam slavery is bound up with the law and institutions of the Coran. Coming, on the other hand, to the Gospel, we find deep down in the doctrine of the Fatherhood of God, the seed which in due time brings forth the fruit of emancipation. For the bondman is the son of a common Father, "not now a slave, but a brother beloved," and as such entitled to a brother's freedom.[1]

Relations of the sexes.

I do not dwell here farther on the relations of the sexes excepting to say that the provisions regarding divorce and servile concubinage have led in Islam to a mass of prurient literature defining the legal conditions of things which ought not so much as to be named—a leaven of corruption. From all this the Christian faith, with its law of monogamy and simple injunction of conjugal fidelity, is altogether free.[2]

Relations of Church to State.

Mahometan nations, following the theocratic model of Islam, have always held Church and State to be one. The secular ruler is the head of the Church, and the form of government is theoretically an absolute and irresponsible despotism. The result has been, through all these long ages, to steadily suppress all attempt at the growth of free institutions. That this might be remedied hereafter in some Mahometan state (such as, for example, some have hoped for in Egypt) is possible; but experience is not favourable to the expectation. From all such dangers the Christian system, which renders to Cæsar the things that be

[1] Philemon 16. [2] 1 Cor. vii. 3.

Cæsar's, is altogether free. Again, there is perhaps no greater contrast in the precepts of the two religions than that relating to the sword. As an instrument for the propagation of the faith (however much practice may have often widely differed from precept), the use of the sword is distinctly abjured by the gospel,[1] while it is as directly commanded by the Coran. Before the Flight, Mahomet was profuse in his declarations that there should be "no constraint in religion." But so soon as he came to power he drew the sword, never, as the reader knows, again to sheathe it; and his followers have not been slow to tread in his steps. "My kingdom," said Jesus Christ to the Roman governor, "is not of this world: if My kingdom were of this world, then would My servants fight, that I should not be delivered to the Jews: but now is My kingdom not from hence."[2]

Use of the sword in propagation of the faith.

Turning now to the spiritual aspect of the two faiths, a wide difference exists between the ordinances of Islam, rigidly tied down as they are to time, and in one respect to place, and those of the Gospel, which can be suited to the changing circumstances of the moment, and the varying demands of clime and season. The obligation to pray in stereotyped ritual at so many stated hours of the day is prone to degenerate into a lifeless worship, though we are far from asserting that it is always so. Much the same may be said of fasting and pilgrimage, the latter being an ordinance practically unattainable by multitudes, and the former, according to the stringent rule of the Coran, altogether impracticable in some zones of the earth.[3] The contrast with the spirit and precept of the gospel, and the

Fixedness of Ordinances.

[1] Matt. xxxvi. 52; John xviii. 36. [2] *Ibid.*

[3] As where all is day or all is night, or nearly so, in the month of Ramadhân.

simplicity of its two positive ordinances, is too patent to need dwelling on.

Love as a motive power.

Again, while the Coran represents God as Creator, Ruler, and Preserver, the Rewarder of good and evil, and the Hearer of prayer—it nowhere recognizes Him as a Father, much less the Father of our Lord Jesus Christ. The sentiment of the Moslem partakes, therefore, of the fear of a servant more than the love of a son. The office of the Holy Spirit as Regenerator is unknown, and the death and resurrection of Christ are denied. There is thus in Islam nothing answering to the grace of redemption, and consequently the grand power of the Gospel—namely, the love of Christ as a constraining influence—is wanting; nor is there the approach to anything that might supply its place.

Contrast between the persons of the Founders. *Mahomet.*

To put the matter shortly, each religion is an embodiment of its founder. Mahomet sought power; he fought against those who denied his claims; he put a whole tribe to the sword; he filled his harem with women, bond and free; he cast aside, when they had served his purpose, the Jewish and Christian Scriptures, and he engrafted his faith on the local superstition of his birth-place. He did all these things under cover of an alleged Divine authority, but he did no miracle.

Jesus.

The life of Jesus is all in contrast. He spake and taught as one having the inherent authority in Himself; but He could also say, "The works that I do in My Father's name, they bear witness of Me." He was holy, harmless, undefiled. He pleased not Himself. Though rich, He became poor, that we through His poverty might become rich. He made Himself of no reputation, and took upon Him the form of a servant. He was despised and rejected of men. He humbled Himself, and became obedient unto death, even the death of the cross.[1]

Is there any common point whatever in the two lives? "He that is of the earth is earthy, and speaketh of the earth; He that cometh from heaven is above all."

Where in the Coran are to be found words like these, descriptive at once of the new life and of the Giver of it?

> "I am the Resurrection, and the Life: he that believeth in Me, though he were dead, yet shall he live: and whosoever liveth and believeth in Me shall never die."

And again—

> "I am the Good Shepherd: the Good Shepherd giveth His life for the sheep."

And yet again—

> "Come unto Me, all ye that labour and are heavy laden, and I will give you rest. Take My yoke upon you, and learn of Me; for I am meek and lowly in heart: and ye shall find rest unto your souls. For My yoke is easy, and My burden is light."

[1] John v. 36; Rom. xv. 3; 2 Cor. viii. 9; Isa. liii. 3; Phil. ii.

APPENDIX IV.

THE ARABIAN CALENDAR.

Arabian Months	Corresponding Months
Moharram	April
Safar	May
Rabî I	June
Rabî II	July
Jumâd I	August
Jumâd II	September
Rajab	October
Shabân	November
Ramadhân	December
Shawwâl	January
Dzul Cáda	February
Dzul Hijj	March

The Arabian months are lunar, and the year was before Islam made to correspond with the solar, by the intercalation of a month every third year. The reckoning was thus luni-solar until, at the Farewell pilgrimage, Mahomet, by abolishing intercalation, made the Mussulman, or *Hegira*, year a purely lunar one.

This table gives the months as they stood at the time of Mahomet's flight to Medina, and they were so maintained by intercalation with little variation till the Farewell pilgrimage, that is, till close upon the prophet's death.

INDEX.